MW00638588

I DO
(I THINK)

CONVERSATIONS ABOUT MODERN MARRIAGE

Also by Allison Raskin

Overthinking About You

Coauthored with Gabe Dunn

I Hate Everyone But You
Please Send Help

HANOVER
SQUARE
PRESS™

Recycling programs
for this product may
not exist in your area.

ISBN-13: 978-1-335-01251-7

I Do (I Think)

This is a work of creative nonfiction. The events are portrayed to the best of the author's memory.
Some names and identifying details have been changed to protect the privacy of the people
involved.

This publication contains opinions and ideas of the author. It is intended for informational and
educational purposes only. The reader should seek the services of a competent professional for
expert assistance or professional advice. Reference to any organization, publication or website
does not constitute or imply an endorsement by the author or the publisher. The author and the
publisher specifically disclaim any and all liability arising directly or indirectly from the use or
application of any information contained in this publication.

TM and ® are trademarks of Harlequin Enterprises ULC.

Hanover Square Press
22 Adelaide St. West, 41st Floor
Toronto, Ontario M5H 4E3, Canada
HanoverSqPress.com

Printed in U.S.A.

To John,
You're Worth the Risk

I DO
(I THINK)

CONVERSATIONS ABOUT MODERN MARRIAGE

TABLE OF CONTENTS

NOTE TO READER

Before we dive in, I wanted to take a moment to acknowledge the complexities of marriage both on a personal and cultural level. Given these complexities and variations of experiences, it is not a topic that can ever be fully explored in all its detail. So I've limited the scope by primarily examining the legal standards, history, and social norms of marriage in Western society. I also did my best to be as inclusive as possible within that constraint, but it is impossible to ignore my privilege and perspective as a straight, cis woman who has never been forced into marriage culturally or financially. This is not the case for many people, and it would be misleading to imply otherwise. I also want to note that this book does not explore the dynamics of abusive marriages. It didn't feel right for me to take that on without adequate personal or professional experience. (If you or someone you love is in an abusive marriage, please see our resources page.) There are also occasional mentions of violence and suicidal ideation. I hope you are able to read with care and lots of self-compassion.

Finally, this book would not be possible without the dozens of people who opened their hearts and marriages to me. Thank you for answering all my nosey questions.

INTRODUCTION:
FROM THIS DAY FORWARD

If you were to Google the definition of marriage, the dictionary results would be pretty useless. What exactly does Merriam-Webster mean by "the state of being united as spouses in a consensual and contractual relationship recognized by law," when so many aspects of married life have changed since that rather vague definition was written? *How* united are we supposed to be? *What* is appropriate to expect from our contractual spouses? And *why* do so many of these initially consensual contracts end up being unilaterally dissolved? I've often felt that for all the societal, financial, and familial pressures we face in the decision to legally bind our lives to another person, there is not enough pragmatic investigation into what actually makes it work—especially now that it is no longer a social necessity, like in past generations, but a choice.

Books about marriage aren't new. But I do think we are at a turning point for how modern generations conceptualize and feel about what was once an unquestioned, indestructible institution. This doesn't mean marriage is about to go away (or that our society is going to fall into complete anarchy, as some fear-mongering voices would have you believe). Instead, I think our changing world is developing a new relationship toward it. People considering marriage are confronting different variables, timing thresholds, financial realities and social norms, that people twenty years ago may not have had to consider, and it's left them with a lot of uncertainty and differing opinions than past generations.

According to a survey done by the Thriving Center of Psychology, two out of five millennials and Gen Z think that marriage is outdated. While that is a significant percentage, it is still not the majority—and it also doesn't mean they're taking marriage off the table. The researchers found that 83% of those surveyed still hope to get married someday, while 85% don't think marriage is required to have a committed, long-term partnership. Although these results come from a small sample size (906 millennials and Gen Z who are partnered but not married), it touches on an important phenomenon.

Younger generations no longer seem to view marriage as necessary for a successful partnership, but many still want to do it anyway.

This makes me wonder: Why? What continues to make marriage so compelling in today's changing society? And

how will our evolving relationship toward marriage influence what those marriages look like?

Personally, I have wanted to be married my entire life—
to the point where it became an unhealthy fixation. I spent
my twenties desperately trying to lock down a husband,
regardless of our compatibility level or even their overall interest in me. I felt a pressure when I was younger to
get to the next level with my partners so our relationship
would be both societally legitimate and personally safe.
(Two assumptions I will be challenging throughout this
book.) I did not think my adult life would fully start until
I was married and had a partner I could rely on and view
as family. And while part of that mindset was a result of
my own internal biases and issues (more on that later as
well), a lot of it can be traced back to my environment.
We live in a society that so habitually prioritizes and rewards marriage, we often don't think to ask why that is.
Or push back on whether this institution should still hold
the same status in modern times as it has in the past.

I should warn you that despite posing these questions,
this book isn't going to be a takedown of marriage. Instead, I want to engage with and explore the various forms
that marriage can take, and the power we individually
have to shape something that is often, incorrectly, presented as a monolith. I'll be examining the realities of
marriage through many different lenses—legal, emotional,
financial, and crucially, the mental health part of the arrangement, because I can think of few events that are

more anxiety-producing than the decision to marry another human being who can leave you at any moment.

I'll confess that as someone who has had anxiety and OCD since I was a preschooler, a lot of this mental health focus is influenced by my own experience. As I discussed in my other book, *Overthinking About You: Navigating Romantic Relationships When You Have Anxiety, OCD and/or Depression*, our mental health is directly impacted by our relationships and vice versa. And even if you don't have a diagnosed mental disorder or relationship baggage or attachment issues— wild, if true—you can't ignore the mental stakes of legally tying yourself to another person. As younger generations get more comfortable talking about mental health and prioritizing mental wellness, we can finally start to openly acknowledge that getting married comes with a lot of uncertainty.

Did I make the right choice? Will I be happy? Can I emotionally/financially/physically survive a divorce? Am I doing this for me or for someone else (like my mom)?

In 2024, we're officially allowed to ask ourselves these questions out loud because, outside of certain cultures, there are far fewer factors forcing us to get hitched. We get to actually make a pros and cons list instead of shoving our doubt deep inside until it explodes at a Thanksgiving dinner seven years later in front of our friends and family. (No, this did not happen to me, but it's probably happened at least once to someone! Holidays are stressful.)

I'll confess that my personal experiences are a large part of what motivated my investigation in the first place. You see, a month before my thirty-first birthday, I finally got engaged. At that point, I had been with my partner for about fifteen months, but I felt confident in our ability to "go the distance," which to me meant "sticking it out until death." (How romantic!) My dream of finding my forever buddy had actually come true, and I let myself sink into a new sense of security. But six months after he proposed, he left me with what I felt was no explanation other than "something is missing." To say I was surprised would be an insulting understatement. I was shocked, devastated, and thrust into a new reality I had not even considered given the stable nature of our relationship. I only managed to survive that heartbreak due to my support system and newly stable mental health, but it altered something in me.

For so long, I had viewed marriage as an end point, or, for all of you sports fans, the end zone. If I could just make it over the line, I would be safe and partnered for years to come. Obviously, this was a naive point of view. But while I had grown up surrounded by married couples, I didn't have much personal experience with divorce. My parents are still together and my sister married her college sweetheart. While I have friends with divorced parents, it happened before I entered their lives. So as much as I panicked that I would never get married, I always assumed that if it *did* happen, it would be the kind that lasts.

That assumption changed the moment my ex-fiancé walked out. Suddenly, marriage seemed foolhardy and misguided. Why give someone so much power over your life if they might burn it all down? For the first time in my life, getting married no longer felt like a safe oasis—it felt like a risk that maybe wasn't worth taking. But then I met a man named John. And I realized that I didn't want one person's rejection of me to change what I had always wanted for myself. I didn't need to give up on marriage, but it was apparent that I did need to rethink my perspective and relationship with it. If this huge thing was no longer completely good or completely terrifying, what version of it would remain?

It was that question that made me decide to write this book and investigate what it truly means to get married and to stay married in current day, as well as what's now involved in "the marriage conversation." I thought about all the questions I had, and the topics that no one talks about enough, or talked about at all, given how much marriage has evolved in recent years. I faced my own fears and insecurities while asking dozens of couples with totally different backgrounds to share their experiences. I also turned to numerous experts including divorce lawyers, financial advisers, sociologists, and couples therapists for their insights. I was a woman on a mission to demystify this massive institution that seems to be changing as quickly as our opinions about it.

Some of you reading this might already be dating the person you want to marry, some of you might still be considering if marriage is the right decision at all, and some of you might reject the entire concept. Regardless of whether you get married yourself, the marriages we grow up around and the marriages we witness as adults shape how we see the world and possibilities of human connection. And I think that makes modern marriage worth exploring no matter what our individual inclination toward it might be.

I am writing today as someone who has been engaged twice and married once. I do not know if my new marriage will last forever. But I feel far more prepared for whatever is to come, thanks in part to my investigation that I now get to share with all of you. I went into this process unattached to any singular version of marriage and I think the results are stronger for it. I got to ask a bunch of uncomfortable questions and tried to challenge my own harmful biases whenever they popped up. I didn't set out with a hypothesis to prove. I led with genuine curiosity, and I hope it shows.

The process of writing this book brought me a lot of clarity when it comes to my own conceptualization of marriage. I feel more at peace with my decision to get married in the first place, and I am better able to articulate why it is something I want, even if it isn't something I need. But this isn't all about me. I might be steering the ship, but you are here to draw your own conclusions. I doubt any two people will walk away from this read having had the same internal experience. And that is sort of the point. Modern marriage isn't something we fit ourselves into, it's something we shape around ourselves. No two marriages are identical, which you will soon see through a series of anecdotes sprinkled throughout from people willing to be totally honest with me about their relationships (even when it made us all a *little* uncomfortable).

I am not here to "fix" your marriage, or to convince you not to get married in the first place. I'm here to share what I've learned so you can make a more educated decision if marriage is right for you and, if it is, what *kind* of marriage you want to have. It's always better to know what you are looking for than get sucked into something that is just going to waste your time or break your heart. I have also enlisted experts to share advice on how to navigate your marital journey more smoothly and tips for how to deal with the possibility that your marriage might not last forever. Because it's not enough to just start these conversations without giving you something substantive and useful to walk away with.

After years of romanticizing marriage, I now view it as a calculated risk. I think there are ways to mitigate that risk, as you will soon read, but it is impossible to make it go away completely. I can't promise that after reading this book, your current marriage or future union will be able to withstand any threats or hardships. I can't promise that you will get to die in each other's arms after decades of uninterrupted love and companionship. Or that you will know for sure, without a doubt, that you are not the marrying kind. But I do think we will all walk away a bit more prepared for one of the biggest decisions of our lives. And hopefully be able to coherently explain why we made that decision in the first place.

1

A (SPARKNOTES) HISTORY OF MARRIAGE

Is It As Bad As We Think?

While we all have awful memories of 2020, one noticeably absent part was having to travel all over the world to attend a myriad of weddings. According to the Institute for Family Studies, the pandemic caused a dip in marriages for 2020 and 2021. But this trend didn't last long: what soon followed was a bulk of backlogged weddings as everyone scrambled to *finally* tie the knot in 2022. During the prevaccine era of the pandemic, couples were not only forced inside, but they also had to wait to access the long-promised benefits of marriage: shared health insurance, the ability to make medical decisions for a partner, and legal protections for any nonworking spouse. And worst of all, they had to wait painfully long to get a bunch of gifts and attention.

To be fair, we didn't exactly need a global pandemic to recognize the ways in which our society rewards marriage. Single people don't exactly get to send out registries when they move into a new house or turn a certain age. And no one congratulates you or throws you a party for living with the same platonic roommate for twenty years. (Although, I would argue that is quite a feat, especially if you have tandem parking.)

Yet despite all the glitz and glamour that comes with it, a study by the *National Center for Family & Marriage Research* has shown a steep decline in marriages since the 1970s. So why the sharp decline if matrimony is really as wonderful and beneficial as the federal government and most religions would have you believe? Great question. I want us to take a journey into the ways marriage has evolved from an unquestionably necessary tradition to what many could argue it is now: an unnecessary status symbol that mostly benefits rich white people.

As a financially privileged white person, I'll admit that until I took on writing this book, I went out of my way to avoid looking into the seedier or more problematic elements of marriage because, quite frankly, I didn't want to know. I've suspected in the back of my mind that being so fixated on marriage was at odds with the rest of my progressive views. I also had a vague sense that marriage had patriarchal origins, and that involving the government in your relationship wasn't inherently romantic. Still, I was reluctant to dive into the whole truth. What if I uncovered something that made me feel guilty or uncomfortable for taking part in a problematic institution? Would I have to reassess my whole life plan? Could I still ask my family to spend an exorbitant amount of money on one single day without feeling like I had simply been duped by the wedding industrial complex (which took in approximately $70 billion dollars in 2023)?

Now, denial has its place (like when you find a hair in your food at a restaurant and convince yourself it's from your own head, or you avoid reading a defamatory article about your favorite skin care brand so you can keep using it). But how could I feel sure that marriage didn't conflict with my values if I didn't understand what I was signing up for? I don't think it'd be productive for any of us to enter a legal union without fully comprehending its history, and thus, its legacy.

That said, while it is easy to worry that we are part of a larger societal problem simply by *desiring* matrimony, I think it's important to delineate between the unions of yesteryear, what it means to get married today, and how we hope marriage will evolve in the future. Not to shock any of you, but as you'll soon read, marriage doesn't have the best résumé when it comes to equal rights or the patriarchy. So how do we separate the type of marriage we want today from its uglier, outdated forms? Can we, both individually and collectively, figure out how to keep the fish *and* spit out the bones (or some other less horrifying metaphor)? The optimist in me likes to think so. And the realist in me happens to agree too.

To help me navigate the roots of marriage, I turned to two sociologists (and one marriage equality expert) for their insights. When I asked Jennifer Randles, PhD, a professor and chair of the Sociology Department at California State University, Fresno, why marriage was created in the first place, she quickly warned me that it's a "very unromantic answer." One of the biggest purposes, much as we see in shows like *Game of Thrones*, was to consolidate power and resources between families. She explained that before mass urbanization and industrialization, you didn't go get food from the supermarket or buy your clothes from a store. Your family unit was basically your entire economy, so it made sense you would want to expand that economy to include other families and combine resources through marriage. If you think that sounds more like a corporate merger than a romantic declaration of two souls becoming one, you're not wrong. Having children was a way to expand your business and consolidate wealth with other families. If you didn't procreate, you couldn't grow.

Arielle Kuperberg, PhD, an associate professor of Sociology and Women's, Gender and Sexuality Studies at University of North Carolina Greensboro, agreed with this sentiment. She even harkened all the way back to hunter-gatherers when marriage was theorized to be a sort of survival mechanism. Tribes would exchange spouses with other tribes to build ties and alliances. Arielle explained, if two tribes ran into each other while trying to gather a limited number of apples, instead of fighting to the death over the resource, tribe members could protect themselves by saying, "my sister married a guy in that tribe, there's my sister right there!" Suddenly, this other tribe wasn't a threat because you were connected to them by marriage and bloodlines.

Even as people moved away from hunting and gathering and began owning land, marriage continued to serve a purpose in people's survival and quality of life. People would marry their child off to a family who had adjoining land with the idea being that in time "they'll inherit both farms and make it one giant farm," which would ensure their children were prosperous. For centuries, marriage was an economic partnership, and if you happened to actually like or love your spouse, that was more of a fun bonus.

You might also be surprised to learn that the religious component of Christian marriage started rather late in its evolution. Elements like prayer were added to the wedding ceremony only after 300 AD, and marriage only became a sacrament in the Catholic Church as a result of the Council of Trent in 1547. Jewish people, however, seem to have always viewed marriage as tied to their religious experience, and marriage is mentioned favorably in the Torah. Similarly, Islam promotes marriage and views it as a blessing. While marriage remained unromantic for centuries, it didn't remain nonreligious, giving it an added significance for many families.

So, when did marriage start to shift toward the more

personal? Jennifer explained to me that prominent sociologist Andrew Cherlin believes marriage has evolved through three major phases in more recent history. The first was the institutional economic relationship during the nineteenth century and prior, which we already touched on. The second was a shift in the mid-1800s into "what's often called a *companionate marriage*." This wasn't a complete departure from its first iteration. There were still "gendered divisions of labor" and economic reasons for the arrangement. But there was a new focus on the emotional and relational satisfaction through the companionship that marriage can bring.

It was only once we hit the mid-1960s that the idea of *self-expressive marriage* became more popular. Cherlin's third phase, according to Jennifer, includes a new sentiment that sounds more like, "I'm going to get married because this is a way for me as an individual to become individually fulfilled. And if I'm not happy as an individual, then that justifies me getting a divorce." This type of thinking about marriage didn't really exist before, because, for most of human history, divorce wasn't really an option. Suddenly, marriage was allowed to serve you as an independent person, and not just your entire extended family (or God).

Along with the popularization of divorce, other changes had to take place in Western society for us to be able to move from "marriage is a necessary business deal" to "marriage is a choice that should enrich my life." Until the 1970s, adult women struggled to exist on their own without a husband. As Jennifer explained, it was a challenge to get mortgages or credit cards "in their own names without a husband being a cosigner." In many ways, women's quality of life was intrinsically tied to their marital status. And while that is no longer technically true, I think the residual effects of that reality remain in our societal subconscious. A single woman can have an amazing career, a large group of friends, and a gorgeous rescue dog, and people will still tend to assume that her life is somehow worse than that of a married woman.

Historically speaking, marriage has been pretty high on the list of patriarchal institutions. Ever wonder about the tradition of women taking their husband's last name? Many trace it back to an English legal doctrine, called coverture, that basically merged a woman's identity with that of her new husband. Back in the day, a married woman couldn't even be charged with a crime because legally she didn't really exist. Yet, despite this sexist history, around 70% to 80% of heterosexual married women still change their names, which, quite frankly, blows my mind. And it's not just the frequency with which modern women change their name, it's the mindset around the choice I find perplexing.

You can have a conversation with someone about equal childcare responsibilities, a man doing all the cooking or even a woman being the sole earner and people will be like "Sounds great! Love that!" But as soon as you suggest that a man take a woman's last name, most people are like, "WHOA! Slow down. That will *never* happen!" Or at least that's how those conversations went for me when I launched a (failed) campaign to get my husband to become a Raskin. (Who wouldn't want to be a Raskin?!) My own mother laughed when I suggested it. *That is simply not done.* But why the hell not? It makes no sense for me to change my name. Not to brag, but I am the one with a Wikipedia page and an Instagram check mark! And yet we will forever have to clarify that we are in fact married when checking into places or picking our dogs up from the vet, because John couldn't possibly break tradition. That is how powerful the remnants of earlier (patriarchal) forms of marriage remain in liberal Los Angeles. At least I found a guy who didn't force me to renounce my Jewish heritage to present like a British aristocrat. (Allison Blakeslee would be a little much, even if I did go to boarding school in Connecticut.)

In talking to Jennifer, I realized just how many modern-day wedding rituals bear the lingering by-products of viewing wives as property. For example, the tradition of the bride's family paying for the wedding is basically a modern-day dowery—even if we don't explicitly think of it that way anymore. Jennifer often asks her students, "Does anyone know why the father walks the bride down the aisle to the husband? What does that mean?" While it might seem harmless or even romantic, it originally symbolized the passage of ownership of the bride from father to husband. (Joke's on my dad—he is never getting rid of me! I will be calling him about insurance plans until one of us dies.)

I know it can feel uncomfortable to learn that a moment you always dreamt about or remember fondly has such misogynist undertones. It makes me wonder if ascribing a new meaning to that moment might help mitigate the discomfort. As a cultural (if not religious) Jew, I had both my parents walk me down the aisle, as is the custom. But instead of seeing it as passing of ownership, I saw it as symbolizing that their years of unending support got me to a place where I was ready to be married. They helped me down the aisle, but they also helped me become the best version of myself. That sits much better with me than the idea of being "handed off" for someone else to deal with. (Feel free to steal that symbolism for yourself if it feels right!)

Luckily, as time has progressed, many factors over the last century—feminist movements, more women in the workforce, the increased availability of divorce—have helped combat some of the more insidious (and sexist) parts of marriage. Does this mean that marriage has evolved into something that is easier to get behind than its previous iterations? Yes and no. The patriarchal nature of marriage hasn't simply evaporated now that women can have financial freedom with or without a spouse. Instead, it just appears in less blatant ways than before.

One of those ways is through the gender norms built into modern-day partnerships. Jennifer believes that in heterosexual marriages, "getting married tends to be associated with more unpaid labor in the home for women"—

i.e., the majority of housework and childcare. In 2021, the Bureau of Labor found that, on average, women spend 47 more minutes on domestic chores each day than men. While that might only sound like the length of one good podcast episode, it adds up to approximately 285 more hours of labor a year. What creates this unfair disparity? One explanation Jennifer offers is that, whether consciously or unconsciously, "marriage tends to have a very traditionalizing influence on people in relationships." Just the reality of being married can cause people to sink more into those traditionally gendered roles. Something along the lines of, *you clean the sink while I pay the bills*. (Even if the woman also made the money to pay those bills…)

Some of you might be reading this and thinking, "Well, I wouldn't allow that sort of unequal dynamic to exist in my marriage!" Which is a totally legitimate reaction. While this is a pattern, it isn't a law of nature that must be obeyed. Research has repeatedly shown that same-sex couples and couples with nonbinary partners have fewer power imbalances and unequal labor divisions than heterosexual marriages. That said, studies can only tell us so much. Even if something is statistically significant, it doesn't mean it applies to all couples everywhere. And of course, there's also variation within queer couples. Some, for example, might intentionally assign more domestic tasks to whomever does less paid labor. While others might gravitate toward certain gender norms subconsciously. All this to say, perhaps marriage itself isn't the issue, so much as the expectations we bring to it.

Knowing that this type of unfair dynamic is possible should encourage all of us, regardless of our sexuality, to have more open conversations around the division of labor in the home. While it may sound obvious, we often forget that we don't have to accept an arrangement that doesn't work for us. Take Jennifer, for example: in her first marriage, her husband told her, "Oh, well, you should do more housework because your standards of cleanliness are higher." That marriage did not last. Meanwhile, her relationship with her current husband is very egalitarian, and she shared that she wouldn't have married him if it wasn't.

Sometimes it can be enough to simply have awareness about these ingrained social norms and tendencies. Just knowing that we are at higher risk of falling into more gendered roles after getting married can allow us to be on high alert for any dynamics that don't sit right or feel true to the kind of marriage we signed up for. I think it also means we need to have direct conversations *before* getting married so we can learn each other's expectations. If your partner grew up in a house where the women cleaned after Thanksgiving dinner while the men watched TV, it's probably useful to know if they plan to continue that tradition, or if they intend to live in a home that's different and less traditionally gendered than the one they came from.

To be clear, neither answer is wrong. There are plenty of people who thrive in traditional gender roles, my sister and her husband included. What we want to avoid is matching up with someone who wants a different type of marriage than the one you are looking for. I know plenty of women who wouldn't feel comfortable being married to a stay-at-home dad. I also know plenty who would sign up for that arrangement in an instant. What's great about being married in 2024 instead of 1954 is that both options are more widely accepted than before.

In my own marriage to John, our domestic chores aren't set in stone. Our responsibilities fluctuate based on who has more on their professional plate. If I'm on a double book deadline, he steps up and cleans the dishes every morning. And if he's working nonstop to turn in a script, I'll take the dogs on their afternoon walk even if I also took them out in the morning. We try (our best) not to keep score or assume that things will be 50/50 all the time. Someone is always going to be doing a bit more. What makes that tolerable is when that someone changes regularly. That said, each of us is still allowed to have exceptions for what we aren't willing to do. (I, for one, rarely take out the trash, even if it's overflowing. But I blame that more on my contamination OCD than a belief that it's "unfeminine.") I also know that if we ever have kids, it will become even more important for us to continue conversations about who is doing what and who needs more support, because I've heard babies can be quite the handful.

Here's another question to consider as we confront the not-so-pretty realities of modern marriage. What *type* of people is getting married today? According to a bunch of flashy research studies, it seems to be those from the happy, healthy and wealthy variety. If you frequent the internet, it's likely you've encountered at least one provocative headline about this, maybe something along the lines of the *Atlantic*'s August 2023 article "Why Are Married People Happier Than The Rest of Us?" Or, from the *Washington Post* in 2015: "Middle age is slightly less terrible when you're married." (Not quite as inspiring, but surefire clickbait.)

While these statements seem like a clear victory for marriage PR, Jennifer raises a crucial question: "Is there something about marriage that makes people happier, healthier, or wealthier? Or is it that happier, healthier, and wealthier people are more likely to get married?" I'll admit this possibility hadn't even occurred to me before our conversation. I, like many, tend to read a headline from a reputable news organization and think: *that sounds correct and must not be significantly more complicated!* But I quickly learned there is evidence supporting a theory about what comes first: marriage or money. At least, according to the Institute for Family Studies, "Americans with more income and assets are more likely to marry and to stay married."

This shift toward marriage becoming more of a stark class divider makes sense when you stop to think about it. As we know, previously people got married for financial reasons, like consolidating wealth or having more manpower to work the family farm. Now, there is an under-current of the opposite: rather than marrying to achieve more financial stability, the common sentiment seems to be that you shouldn't get married until you already are financially stable on your own. The wealth gap doesn't just influence retirement savings or medical care, but also, apparently, our deepest emotional partnerships and decisions around them.

Jennifer explains that when people determine "marriageability," i.e., one's readiness for marriage, they tend to define it for themselves and for potential partners in mostly economic terms. Unlike previous generations, more people want to have an established career, the ability to afford a home, and to have paid off all their debts *before* getting married. And given economic inequality in America, those goals are unfortunately not attainable for many tax brackets. So what ends up happening, according to Jennifer, is a lot of people living in poverty who might think to themselves, "'I'm not marriageable' or 'I haven't met anyone who's marriageable'" because the concept of marriage has become so wrapped up in middle- and upper-class ideals.

As a result of this type of thinking and social construction, Arielle says that the people who are most likely to get married nowadays are people who already have a lot of socioeconomic and educational privilege, and adding "married" to their résumé is like the jewel in the crown of that privilege. And if it's true that the ones tying the knot are likely to already belong to a wealthier class, this all suggests a perpetuating cycle, because married people can then accumulate wealth more easily by combining their resources. So, while it might seem responsible to wait until you are "marriage ready," being overly cautious can also harm your growth potential. Not to mention it is a mental and emotional bummer to feel like you aren't "good enough" to do something people have been doing for millennia.

This becomes even more obvious when you look at all the expenses tied up even in weddings alone. The average cost of a wedding in America was $35,000 in 2023, according to The Knot. You can't spend that kind of money in one day unless you have a lot of money to begin with. Sometimes, as Jennifer explains, the expectations about what a wedding "should" look like contribute to a lot of low-income individuals not getting married. Perhaps they think, "well, unless I can afford a big white wedding, I'm not ready for marriage," especially because we often associate marriage with even larger expenses like home ownership and having kids. Meanwhile, all the things that make a marriage actually fulfilling and successful, like partnership, support, and mutual respect, don't necessarily overlap with your financial status.

This all ties back into some of the ickiness (and capitalism) of marriage culture. It's hard not to think this whole institution might be a sham when people save up for months or longer to purchase a diamond engagement ring, a tradition that only exists in the first place because De Beers, the world's largest diamond company, launched a brilliant ad campaign in 1947. Diamonds don't actually symbolize anything meaningful other than smart marketing (that diamonds, like relationships, were everlasting).

But, despite this dubious rationale, suddenly a person had to be able to spend months of their salary on one piece of jewelry in order to be worth marrying. Even having a white wedding dress is, in its own way, a sign of opulence: as Jennifer explains, it shows everyone that you can afford to wear something once and then never again. The color white only became the norm for a bridal gown in the mid-1800s following Queen Victoria's wedding. And the additional implications around "purity" were only widely attached to the color afterward. Funny how easy it is to forget the history of the things we now take for granted.

While finances continue to play a huge role in wedding planning, as more women become the dominant earner in their family, there is less of a need for them to get married for economic security. Yet it remains an important goal for many people, which suggests the appeal of marriage has shifted somewhat from practical to symbolic. Matrimony has become a figurative transition that shows the world you have officially reached "adult status" and that you really have your shit together. After all, as Arielle points out, wedded spouses remain "the most socially approved of any type of relationship"—and that social legitimacy is a valuable asset. Marriage has shifted away from being the "foundation of adulthood" in recent decades and has instead become the "icing on the cake of adulthood," that only a select few are able to achieve.

As much as I don't want to admit it, I have definitely fallen for this (flawed) belief system. I remember thinking that as soon as I started wearing an engagement ring people would suddenly view me as an adult. And not just any adult, but an adult who is loved and has her life figured out. I have spent my entire existence meeting people and immediately scanning their left hand to see if they are "taken," so I can form a more accurate concept of their lives. (Or I convinced myself that's what I'm doing.) Whenever I see a stranger eating alone at a restaurant and start to worry that they are lonely or sad, the presence of a wedding ring washes away my fears. It's as though my brain rejects the reality that plenty of people are also miserably married. Writing this now, it's easy to see why I have placed so much value on matrimony, given my idealistic associations with it.

Fortunately, most people's assumptions about married versus unmarried people aren't so extreme anymore. We're collectively moving away from using labels like spinster or old maid. In the words of Jennifer, unmarried people aren't automatically "social pariahs" anymore. This is a positive trend because it allows for more people to get married out of a genuine desire to do so, instead of a fear of social repercussions if they don't. That said, it's not as though all the constricting expectations have vanished. Whereas fifty to a hundred years ago, it might've been strange to not be married by 25, the pressure now starts to appear once you hit your thirties or even early forties. The traditional norms are adapting to the new world order instead of disappearing completely.

Another undeniable reason people marry today is because of how it can socially legitimize their family unit. It's one thing to live together out of wedlock (more on that later) but raising a family without being legally tied to each other hasn't reached the same level of societal acceptance. That doesn't mean people aren't doing it though. *Child Trend* shared statistics from 2016 that show the percentage of children born to unwed parents has been going up in recent decades (at the time of its publication, the percentage was around 40% of children). At face value, learning that more people are having children without getting married first doesn't seem to be that big of a deal. No need to gasp or clutch your pearls, right? But the problem is that this shift doesn't apply to couples across the board. Unsurprisingly, Jennifer notes, class difference and racial inequality are at play, and "children who are born into poverty are much less likely to be born to married parents." This yet again ends up perpetuating inequalities, because, like I mentioned before, single parents can't consolidate resources in the same way married parents can—and so the cycle of having less continues. It is hard to raise a child in any situation, but it is even harder to do it without a partner.

On top of these practical hurdles, unmarried parents are also battling the social stigma of having a child out of wedlock, which can be mentally and emotionally taxing. Though it might be less intense than it was in the past, there is no denying that it still exists. This poses the question if, on some level, it is more socially acceptable to be a divorced parent than a parent who never married in the first place. Jennifer believes this to be true. For example, a single mom who was married at one point in time might be "less tragic to people than a woman who's never been married." There is this sense that at least she *tried* to do life the "right" way.

Nothing proves Jennifer's point that marriage isn't an "equal opportunity institution" more than the seismic effort it took to get the United States to legalize same-sex marriage in 2015. Or the fact that until 1967, interracial marriage was still illegal in some states. For all its pro-marriage propaganda, the U.S. has a disgusting history of denying certain people what should be an intrinsic right. Yet this record of discrimination hasn't stopped activists from fighting. I believe that the relatively recent legalization of same-sex marriage in the United States is a fascinating turning point for the role marriage plays in modern society, as it managed to both change and further cement marriage's place as a coveted institution.

In simpler terms: if marriage is a thing of the past, why did people fight so hard to gain access to it less than ten years ago?

To get a better sense of the history and perspective of this movement, I reached out to Christopher Riano, an attorney and coauthor of the book *Marriage Equality: From Outlaws to In-Laws*. One of the reasons Christopher decided to cowrite his book in the first place was so people in the future didn't think marriage equality just "happened" or was a natural progression of the times. Activists fought for five decades to change laws, both on a state and federal level. And though fifty years seems like a long time, in the course of human history, there are few social justice movements that were able to turn the tide of public opinion so quickly. According to Gallup, only 27% of Americans supported same-sex marriage in 1996, but by the time the Supreme Court ruled in its favor in 2015, the national level of support was at 60%. By 2021, 70% of Americans supported same-sex marriage. I think this trajectory raises the question: Why did activists fight so hard for something that many people view as so overtly heteronormative?

I think the answer once again reflects how much significant value marriage still holds in society. If there wasn't that big of a difference between being married or not being married, clearly fewer people would have mobilized around this issue. But there is—and the reality is that even in states where domestic partnership offers the same legal and financial benefits, it still didn't have the same social legitimacy as marriage. Denying a large portion of the population access to a coveted and powerful institution sent a strong message that those populations are still viewed as "other" by the state. Not to mention the fact that certain areas of the country wouldn't recognize your domestic partnership at all if you moved or even visited one of them.

For Christopher, the fight for marriage equality wasn't so much about the right to marry but the right to have the decision in the first place. He points out that it's as a core liberty to "allow people to fit their relationship into what makes the most sense for them." And for some, that is a traditional marriage arrangement. Unsurprisingly, his research consistently reflected that the majority of people at least want the option to partake in a tradition that can both define and bring structure to one of their most important relationships.

Throughout our interview, Christopher repeatedly used the word "dignity" when referring to the marriage equality debate, which I think gets to the heart of why it was such an injustice to deny certain people the ability to marry. Christopher believes his long-term partner has no desire to get married, but he said, "The idea that that option wouldn't exist for those who do want it seems very undignified, very improper in a society that values the individual liberties of its members… You should be able to find ways to protect your most intimate relationships, and you should be able to ensure that the government and that others respect that dignified intimate, personal choice. And you should have the opportunity to make that choice." Indeed, denying access to marriage is distinctly *un*-American if we buy into the notion that America was supposedly founded on the basis of individual rights.

Strangely enough, one unexpected offshoot of the marriage equality movement has been an expansion of relationship options for everyone. Christopher explains that instead of reinforcing the binary of married or not married, this fight has allowed all couples, regardless of their gender or sexual identity to "have access to various different legal structures around the United States." For example, domestic partnership used to be available only for same-sex couples (or couples over 62) in California, but now any couple in the state can choose that option (though marriage is still the only arrangement that offers the same recognized rights federally and state to state).

Now, one could theorize that the relatively quick change in acceptance toward marriage equality was born from a patriotic desire to right a wrong. But one could also wonder, was legalizing same-sex marriage a way to "normalize" or even control queer relationships? If certain people had difficulty understanding or respecting a romantic relationship between two gay men, would that change once they became spouses because that arrangement comes within a known structure and set of expectations? Does legalizing same-sex marriage make queer relationships potentially less threatening to certain people because they are now abiding by the historically heterosexual "rules" of matrimony? I'm not suggesting some grand conspiracy here, but I do wonder if this type of thinking had a subconscious effect on changing people's views.

Somewhat similarly, Jennifer noted that the fight for marriage equality "is still based on a set of laws that are legitimizing one type of relationship over all others"—

thereby forcing many dynamic, diverse relationships to fit into single norm. For example, marriage requires people to pair off in twos in order to get legal recognition, even if they are part of a larger, polyamorous relationship structure. Jennifer reiterates, "What we've tended to do with marriage is allow more people access to it, whether it's interracial couples or same-sex couples. What we've tended to do less is have a larger, more robust effort to make our family laws and our family policies depend less on marriage as the kind of relationship that we hold above all others."

This elevation of marriage is a problem for multiple reasons, because as we know well by this point in the chapter, not everyone has the same level of access to it—legally or financially. The fight for true marriage equality didn't end with the federal legalization of same-sex marriage, and it is impossible to ignore the classist, ableist and patriarchal forces at play when it comes to who can get married easily and what those marriages end up looking like. By protecting and promoting marriage above everything else, we are continuing to create unfair divisions among the population and prevent people from prioritizing other relationships.

Although it isn't talked about enough, there also remains a sizable portion of the population that still doesn't have equal rights when it comes to matrimony. While the option may not have been outlawed for disabled people in the same way as it was for other populations, for a significant number of them, getting married would ruin their lives. (If you have no idea what I'm talking about, prepare to be outraged!) To this day, there are discriminatory laws in place that financially penalize certain disabled people if they get married. Many kinds of disabilities or circumstances qualify adults to receive federal benefits including Supplemental Security Income (SSI). And many people need these benefits to help cover living and medical expenses. But if a disabled adult marries, they could lose some—or all—of these monetary benefits because their partner's income is now taken into account as well, and you have to be below a certain (extremely low) income threshold to remain eligible.

Ultimately, these absurd laws and regulations result in a lot of people not being able to marry their partners even if they want to, because they can't risk a loss of or reduction in their Social Security stipends and health care. Fortunately, there is an active fight to change this major inequality both by disability activists and some members of government, although it has yet to catch the same national attention as other movements. The fact that these barriers exist in the first place, though, further proves that marriage currently functions more like a privilege in this country and not as an equal basic right like it should.

It's disheartening that for all the work done to allow more people to get married, the problems with the institution don't stop there. Legal strides have also had to be taken to help keep people safe once they *are* married, particularly in cases of abuse that occur between spouses. According to the Violence Policy Center, women are more likely to be murdered by a romantic partner than anybody else in the world. Marital rape wasn't even considered a crime until states started changing their laws to address this major problem in the 1970s. And it took until 1993(!) for it to be recognized as a crime in all 50 states. I have to assume the frequency and legal acceptance of marital rape for most of the twentieth century was another remnant of wives being viewed as property by their husbands instead of fully realized people with the right to say no. It's another strike against an institution that fails to include and safeguard all citizens in the ways it should.

If you are finishing this chapter feeling incredibly yucky about your desire to get married right about now, you are not alone. My stomach was in knots when I really thought about my own complicity in buying into this social order and all of its ugly baggage while writing this book. But owning and examining discomfort is a crucial part of growth. Or at least, that's what all my therapists have told me.

So now that we know more about the nitty-gritty details of this massive institution, where does that leave us? Are there ways to engage with marriage without cosigning its more harmful history? Is there enough good that comes from this type of union to override the bad? I like to think so. But creating that type of marriage requires more work than simply signing a certificate. There is a certain mindfulness that is necessary so we don't inadvertently fall into detrimental roles and harmful patterns. For many people in today's world, getting married is (and should be) an active choice—not an inevitability. We want to be in touch with *why* we made that choice and why we are continuing to make it day after day.

I also think it is perfectly understandable to *not* want to make that choice. For some people, especially in younger generations, it doesn't feel possible or even desirable to separate the ugly history from the present possibilities. The benefit of no longer needing marriage for quite as many economic and social reasons is that you don't have to come to terms with it if you don't want to. You can easily live a full and satisfying life without ever getting hitched.

But for those who are still interested, I think it is crucial to acknowledge, even just internally, the privilege that marriage provides, rather than to ignore it and bury our heads in our huge white gowns. We can become proactive about shifting and shaping this institution into something more equitable both on an individual and societal level even just by changing the way we talk and think about it.

In the spirit of entering more thoughtfully into marriage, or providing possible maintenance on your current one, I'm going to end each chapter with some questions to ask yourself and some questions to ask your partner that are inspired by what we just covered. The goal of these exercises is not to automatically know the answers right away but to spark discussions that will hopefully make us more prepared and aligned for what lies ahead.

So without further ado:

QUESTIONS TO ASK YOURSELF

- Is marriage something I genuinely want for myself? Or is it something that is expected of me? If so, from whom? Society? My family? My friend group?
- What rituals, religious or secular, do I want included in my wedding ceremony and what rituals don't sit right with me?
- Do I think married people are more "adult" than unmarried people? If so, is this an assumption I want to challenge?
- How do I feel about traditional gender roles within a couple? Why do they work or not work for me?

QUESTIONS TO CONSIDER WITH YOUR PARTNER

- Are we going to have the same last name? If so, why is that important to us and how are we going to determine whose name is changing and whose name is staying the same?
- How do we think our relationship will change once we are married?
- What parts of our relationship do we *not* want to change once we are married?
- Are there any parts of the institution of marriage that don't feel right to us? What traditional parts do

we not want to keep? (e.g. assuming the woman in a heterosexual marriage will do most of the child-care.)

- Symbolically, what does marriage mean to us?
- Practically, what type of marriage do we want to create together and how are we going to do that?

It's normal if these types of conversations feel over-whelming and scary at first. You don't need to hammer all of this out right away or the second you get engaged. But it could be useful to at least touch on these topics when you're in a good headspace and have a few hours to chat. And if you're currently single and thinking of mingling with marriage, it never hurts to have a firmer understanding for yourself of what you are looking for in the future.

Okay, the history of marriage is officially over. It's time to get a bit more personal.

2
I TAKE YOU
(WHOEVER YOU ARE)

The Big Questions Around
Picking a Spouse

I think we've all heard the phrase "when you know you know," and maybe that really is true for some very neurotypical, eerily calm people. But for the rest of us, the decision of who to marry—or if we even want to get married at all—can be filled with doubt and second-guessing. Especially now that we have far more options for partners than ever before due to a little thing called the internet.

Surprisingly having the choice to marry outside our preexisting social circles hasn't resulted in the kind of "cross pollination" that you'd expect. As much as Western, and more specifically, American culture has transitioned into focusing on love-based marriages, the reality is that *love* isn't the only thing driving our spousal selection. We tend to turn our noses down at traditions like arranged marriages, perhaps because they prioritize the more unromantic factors of compatibility over our feelings. But we often don't realize that we do the exact same thing in less explicit ways.

Put simply, dating apps haven't transformed partner selection as many thought it would. Instead, the use of apps have often resulted in choice overload with participants being overwhelmed by a vast number of options. For many people, this can cause burnout and an inability to make decisions because there are simply too many people for our brains to properly process. Dating apps have also created a culture of *but what if I find someone better* wherein people overlook the good match in front of their face for the possibility of an even greater find. The idea that *one more swipe* might change your life makes it harder to put your phone down and actually commit. This mindset has led to a pattern of people treating apps more like a game to be won rather than the useful resource it can be when used productively. And as someone who has found not one but two fiancés through Hinge, I can assure you they can be quite effective when used correctly. (Even if one of those two fiancés walks out on you later.)

When dating through apps first started to become mainstream around 2012 with the advent of Tinder, Jennifer explained that many people thought apps would "revolutionize marriage and…who partners with whom." While apps changed a lot of aspects of modern dating, the mentality behind our partner selection doesn't seem to be one of them. It seems as if instead we've only technologically reinforced our long history of "same marriage" or "homogamy" where we "marry people who are very much like us" in terms of our background and education level.

So why do we do this? Historically, the tendency has made sense, because we often lived near, worked with, and interacted mostly with people who had similar backgrounds to us, thanks to factors such as residential segregation and institutionalized racism. Dating apps initially seemed like a way for people who didn't have any similar social circles to meet and pair up. But then the interface of the apps allowed for more and more selectivity when it came to whom users were willing to interact with, which basically threw that outcome out the window. Jennifer explains that "because people can express preferences for the racial or ethnic identity of one's partner, their education level, their political affiliations, their religious backgrounds…online dating has in many ways exacerbated these homogamous trends" and "reinforced those patterns of like marrying like."

You might *think* you are having an open mindset by expanding your search from 10 miles away to 20. But it's still unlikely you will swipe right on someone from a completely different socioeconomic background or education level—even if you don't consciously realize it. So sure, maybe our dating pool is theoretically larger now thanks to apps. We're no longer limited to our next door neighbors, coworkers, or our friends' college friends who likely have a somewhat similar upbringing and life résumé to you. But more options don't protect us from being influenced by things like a dating app's algorithms or interface. Or larger societal factors that continue to encourage us to pair up with someone of a similar tax bracket or education level. I mean, I thought I was being wild and adventurous whenever I matched with someone who didn't work in the entertainment industry! That's how warped our (my) perceptions of "different" are.

One of the wildest parts of having met John on Hinge is how easily I could not have met John at all. And I don't mean that in the "what if his profile had never come across my screen" sense. I mean it in the "I almost swiped left, but at the very last second swiped right" sense, due to the expectations I'd set for the kind of person I wanted to be with. My concern wasn't his photos or general vibe, but his career. It said "TV writer" and I had sworn to myself that I wasn't going to date anyone else with that job. I had liked the fact that my ex-fiancé wasn't in the entertainment industry, and I was looking for the same thing in my next relationship. Having had a partner with a "traditional job" added a level of stability to my life. One of us was always going to have a paycheck coming in. One of us was always going to have health care benefits. Also, a lot of people in Los Angeles identify as "writers" but are actually "aspiring writers" or they write without getting paid to write. And while there's nothing wrong with that—it is very freakin' hard to actually get paid to write—I was personally at a stage in my life when I wanted someone who was at least somewhat established in their field. Otherwise, I knew my own stress about living a freelance lifestyle would double.

But then I looked at the profile again. And I noticed something that made me want to give him a shot. In one of his responses to a prompt, he said something along the lines of, "Do gingerbread men ever freak out when they realize they are living in a house made of their own flesh?" I found that joke so funny that I swiped right. Yes. A dark joke about a gingerbread man is the reason I now have a life partner. To be fair, a good sense of humor has always been one of my top priorities! And one of the unique aspects of online dating is that you can be more discerning up front with the information in front of you rather than trying to piece together key details through a conversation. This ability can either reinforce one's unhelpful pickiness *or* weed out unsuitable candidates faster. (Or both!) In my case, Hinge almost caused me to skip John because it revealed his career, but I also got a sense of his humor through one of the prompts, which for me is a necessary quality in a partner. That is a lot of information to gather about a stranger before even interacting with them!

He and I matched later that day and immediately started chatting back and forth before setting up a FaceTime call that weekend. I was still recuperating from my broken engagement at my parents' house in New York while John was in Los Angeles, so the first month of our relationship was long distance. While we had obvious chemistry, or as much chemistry as one can detect over a screen, we weren't "safe" or "smart" choices for each other. I was barely three months out from having my life blown apart. And John, while an actual TV writer and not just an aspiring one, was unemployed. He was in development on two promising projects, but didn't have a source of income at the moment.

So I had a tough choice to make. Was his career instability going to be a deal-breaker for me? Or did other things—such as our effortless banter and his ability to understand my abandonment wound—matter more? One factor that helped me decide was discovering we had a mutual friend who not only vouched for John, but sang his praises. Knowing someone who liked him in real life helped me feel more comfortable getting to know him virtually. And by the time I returned to Los Angeles, we were basically a couple even though we had never met in person. I had betrayed my original intentions by deciding to date a struggling writer, but from where I'm standing, I also honored them by allowing myself to fall in love with someone who has shown up—and made me laugh—day after day. (For the record, his comedic repertoire extends far beyond cookies having existential crises.)

Beyond the ways our picky preferences can hold us back, another part of partner selection that can be especially elusive is timing—particularly, the timing of where each partner is on their individual journeys. The Allison of today is very different from the Allison of yesteryear, and that impacted what type of relationships I've been able to have. If we had met in our twenties, I don't think John and I would have ended up marrying each other or even dating that seriously. Take, for example, the fact that I don't drink because alcohol tastes disgusting to me, while younger John spent a lot of time socializing at bars and going to wine tastings. This might seem like a nonissue, but in the past he was looking for someone who enjoyed doing those things too. I was—and am—not that person. But by the time we met, John didn't care about that as much anymore and has even become accustomed to my 10:00 p.m. bedtime and preference for an early bird dinner.

Meeting at an older age also meant we were both better at regulating our emotions and communicating directly. It's easy to say given the ease of our relationship that we are "just right for each other" when in reality we are both just better at being partners. Sometimes it's not that we haven't found the "right" partner, it's that we aren't fully ready for the kind of relationship we think we want. (Looking at you, Allison, age 0–29.)

But the question remains: How do we know what to look for? My ex-fiancé had every trait I was told a partner should have. He was kind, funny, and reliable. We didn't jump into our engagement without really knowing each other first. And everyone in my life approved of our relationship. I distinctly remember thinking after we got engaged: *this is a good choice, Allison. This person is safe and secure. Great work!* And yet... I was left sobbing on the bathroom floor while he packed a backpack with my returned engagement ring in his pocket.

I think my healing would have been easier if I'd learned after the fact that people had questioned my choice of partner. That would bring some sort of logic and a clear error into the picture. Instead, everyone was as baffled by my ex's leaving as I was. They all thought we were a great couple. My parents were thrilled when he called to ask for my hand in marriage. (Another strange, patriarchal tradition I still wanted to participate in, mostly because, if it isn't clear by now, I am obsessed with my parents.) He was objectively a good guy. So when things fell apart, I found myself questioning my judgment. Was I bad at choosing? Or was my broken engagement during a pandemic a fluke that I shouldn't attach much meaning to?

I think we've all known couples who have been together for years and thought, *How can that possibly work?!* And we've all seen relationships end after thinking the couple was a perfect match. It leaves us wondering, what is the magic sauce? Why do some pairings go the distance and others fizzle out or blow up? What really matters when it comes to spouse selection to set us up for success?

In order to get to bottom of these questions, I turned to two therapists for their professional opinions, as well as some real-life love stories from nonlicensed, everyday couples who responded to my open call for interviews for this book. Because sometimes it's as easy as following a certain set of rules to find what you're looking for. And other times…well, you'll see.

As we know, one of the limitations of picking a potential spouse is that we can't just open their brain and figure out exactly who they are on our first date. As Jessica Baum, a licensed mental health counselor and relationship expert, beautifully put it, "We don't meet the whole person in the beginning."

As much as I hate to admit it given my impatient personality, it takes time to actually get to know someone. While it's annoying that we can't figure someone out right away and make the right call after every single first date, I can come to terms with needing time to understand another person. What is harder for me to accept is the possibility that you might *never* be able to fully know someone. And if that's the case, are you effectively signing up to merge your life with a stranger? I sometimes wrestle with this anxiety, and while I was hoping the professionals would be able to calm me down, both Jessica and psychologist Dr. Shelly Collins agreed that I was right: there are always going to be parts of your partner that are unknown. DITH! (That's a Raskin family abbreviation for Damn It to Hell!)

As Dr. Shelly explains, "You can know your partner in so much as they know themselves." Which means, there are parts of ourselves that are unknown even to *us*. Jessica seconded that sentiment with, "People can't share parts of themselves that they have not accessed." For example, I can't completely predict every part of John's response and behavior if we have a child and then lose that child. And neither can he. There are some life experiences that we don't know how we will react to until they happen to us. All we can do, as Dr. Shelly says, is "look at the evidence of how they behaved in other areas of their life."

I think this point speaks to the importance of not just knowing all the facts about someone before you commit to marrying them, but also needing to have experienced the reality of life together. Biographical traits are one thing. Behavioral observation is another.

As people spend time with their partners, they can study the decisions and actions they make to help answers to questions like: *Can I trust this person to meet my emotional needs? If I'm merging finances with them, can I trust their ability to manage money? If I want to have kids, what kind of parent will they be?* And, perhaps, most importantly, *Is this person able and willing to compromise?* Because it doesn't really matter if someone feels like your soulmate if they don't know how to actively be a partner and share their life with you.

Everyone has different personal preferences when it comes to an ideal partner, so it's rather useless to try to put together a universal list of "what to look for" in another person. But I do think it can be helpful to highlight some traits we should all try to avoid.

Dr. Shelly does a particularly great job of identifying qualities that are likely to make a long-term marriage more difficult. Aside from abusive tendencies of any kind, she says you might want to steer clear of someone who says they will change their behavior—be it no longer staying out late or agreeing to take better care of their health—but then consistently doesn't. Add to the list anyone who seems to have an emotional hole they are looking for you to fill, or people with super possessive tendencies. And, if you value monogamy, you should pay attention if they have a habit of being unfaithful. As much as we want to believe otherwise when we're in love, it's unlikely that hurtful behavior is suddenly going to stop if the only new variable is they are now dating you instead of someone else.

Outside of these distinct qualities, Dr. Shelly believes that one of the best ways to figure out what *not* to look for is by examining what didn't work in your past relationships. Maybe you've already learned that you need a super clear communicator, or someone with a strong work-life balance. Certain qualities aren't going to be deal-breakers for everyone, but if you already know they don't work for you, there is no point in repeating history with someone new, even if the excitement of other qualities outweigh those at first. For example, I don't do well with anyone who isn't driven in their chosen career. I also know from experience that I'm not compatible with people who throw costume parties. Equally important to know if you ask me.

It's clear that looking at our own relationship history can help inform our spouse selection—but how much are we supposed to be paying attention to our *partner's* past? When I look back at my relationship with my ex-fiancé, one brief moment stands out to me as a potential red flag. We were on our second date and over Thai food, he told me that following a five-year-long relationship with a camp girlfriend that ended in his early twenties, he hadn't been in anything long-term. Following that relationship, he had chronologically dated one girl for nine months, one girl for six months and one girl for three months. Each time he had been the one to end it—much to their surprise, he admitted. If I were a dog, my ears would have perked up in concern. But since I am merely human, I simply nodded.

At the time, I worried that this was not a good dating pattern. It alluded to a fear of commitment and maybe some residual hang-ups regarding the one that got away. But then again, as I told myself back then, my past patterns weren't anything to write home about. I decided to judge him based on how he acted in our burgeoning relationship instead of how he'd behaved in the past. It was the type of generosity I wanted for myself, so it seemed only fair to extend it to him. And he appeared to have no issue committing to me. So I tucked that information away and didn't give it much thought until he abruptly ended it with me, almost two years later. Now I was the one who was surprised (and devastated). Although I felt weirdly proud that our relationship at least progressed further than his past ones by reaching the engagement benchmark, I felt silly for thinking I wouldn't be a victim of the same outcome as his exes.

Yet, despite how things ended, I still don't regret my decision to give him the benefit of the doubt. While we should pay attention to our potential partner's relationship patterns and history, I don't think it is fair to handcuff them to it, because that doesn't allow for the possibility that people can change. (Speaking as someone who has changed *a lot*.)

Keeping this in mind, Dr. Shelly suggests that instead of outright judging someone for their past and walking away, we should be collecting information from them as though we're detectives or researchers. Sometimes this means directly asking your new partner some tough questions. *Why do they think things didn't work out in their last few relationships?* If they had to guess, *what are their exes' perspectives on why it ended?* I've found this line of questioning has been a pretty great way to get a sense of people's self-awareness and ability to empathize. And if they can point to a behavior that caused issues (like, for example, a little too much flirting), but say they don't do that kind of stuff anymore, maybe it's worth asking, "*Why* don't you do it anymore?" Because as we all know, it's easy to say what people want to hear, but it's harder to actually change without a clear reason or road map.

There is also a big difference between trusting that someone has changed before you met and hoping that they will change in the future. Some of us are too drawn to a person's potential and not their current reality, even without properly realizing it. But choosing someone based on who they *might* become has always seemed like an overly risky endeavor to me. As I've gotten older, I've tried to ask myself, if nothing ever changed, can I take this person as they are? I would want to make sure I'd still be all in if their current self was pretty similar to their future self. It's not a good feeling for either partner if one of them keeps waiting for the other to upgrade—nor is it that likely to ever happen.

Dr. Shelly agrees there is extra risk involved when we focus on potential. I've learned that one way to minimize that risk is to not get too serious until you see your potential partner taking tangible action. So if, early on in a relationship, your partner declares some big intention, like wanting to go back to school to start a new career, maybe it isn't wise to fully commit until they actually take that big step. Or at least take the time to determine if you'll be okay if they *never* take that step.

Potential, at least to me, is almost ethereal. It's impossible to know if someone will ever fully find theirs until it happens. While recognizing your partner's potential can be wonderful and rewarding, it can also become a sticky trap if there isn't also a willingness to accept that they might never reach it. Pasts and futures are important factors for evaluating partners, but at the end of the day, all we have is the person they are right now.

In a 2015 Pew Research Study, participants were asked what factors they believe make a marriage most successful. They found that the most common answer was given by 64% of surveyors, who credit having shared interests. (In the second most popular answer, 61% of people credited a satisfying sexual relationship.) But if shared interests are so indicative of relationship satisfaction, why do we keep being told that opposites attract?

One part of my parents' love story that has always made me laugh is how much my mom didn't want to wind up with someone like my dad. She fancied herself an independent spirit with artistic taste who loved foreign films and wanted to work abroad. My dad was an aspiring accountant from Long Island. For their first date, he asked if she wanted to see *King Kong* and she thought he was joking. He was, as my mom put it, "just not my jam." But despite the differences in their interests, their shared sense of humor, and ease with each other ultimately changed her mind. They recognized how they aligned on big picture stuff, like their principles and politics, and surprised each other in their personal details.

When I first asked my dad how he knew my mom was the person he wanted to marry, his answer got at this same idea. He believes that what makes their marriage work is that they both see things the same way. They might have different backgrounds (my mom's family struggled financially after her father died, while my dad grew up in a quintessential upper-middle-class home). They might have different interests (he's a poker and baseball kind of guy while she loves to knit and discuss Russian literature). But they agree on what it means to live a good life and have had the same long-term goals and priorities. And I think this speaks to a deeper kind of compatibility than sharing a favorite ice cream flavor. (Which they don't.)

That said—as my mother was quick to point out—no

two people are going to move through the world in *exactly* the same way. Yes, they agreed on how to tackle all the major stuff like finances, children, politics, and religion (Jewish-lite), which made navigating their 45-year-marriage easier than most. But they also have fundamental differences in their personalities that continue to rub each other wrong. My dad is a classic type A go-getter while my mother avoids making phone calls like they're the plague. One of their earliest fights happened simply because my mother failed to have an opinion about something, while my father couldn't imagine someone not having an opinion about everything. But these types of differences haven't torn them apart because they still don't get in the way of the aforementioned "major stuff."

And, as Dr. Shelly points out, "You're not dating yourself." Considering we are two completely separate people, we can't expect our partner to operate the same way as we do, or judge them by the same rubric we use to judge ourselves—even if we really want to. Just ask my dad, who still struggles to understand why my mom hates making phone calls—four and a half decades later. Something that has helped me when I start to feel irritated that John isn't just an Allison duplicate in a male body, is realizing how *wonderful* it is that John isn't an Allison duplicate in a male body. While my brain has a lot of strengths, it also has weak areas that…could use some help. And that's where having another brain around comes in handy when you're doing life together.

Regardless of whether opposites attract, I think the

more important question is, can true opposites stay happily married? Because it is one thing to get into a fiery debate when you first start dating, and it is another to discover that you're bumping heads every day for the rest of your life. I think a lot of it comes down to how you view these seemingly incompatible inclinations. Basic personality differences—from different driving techniques to different reactions in a crisis—can make you both stronger. Especially if partners approach their differences with understanding instead of judgment. Separate interests also push us out of comfort zones and keep life more exciting. But if our different preferences end up becoming a source of constant tension, it will probably be clear early on, and it might be worth finding a different partner who also likes what we like. (Even if you have varying skill levels. For example, I have yet to beat John at tennis.)

As much as we like to think of marriage as a special dyad that exists in its own universe filled with inside jokes and pillow talk, the reality is that unless you are trapped on a desert island with just your spouse, other people play a role in your relationship. Even though John and I met midpandemic and prevaccine, which had a certain desert island effect, I eventually had to meet the other loved ones who populate his world. And he had to get used to me FaceTiming my parents multiple times a day. If you don't want your relationship to exist in a vacuum, as you become more serious, you have to begin to integrate your new partner into the rest of your life.

This ability to join each other's communities is important because when you partner with someone, Jessica notes, "They're not eliminating your world and you're not eliminating theirs. You're creating a co-world together." I love this conceptualization because we often talk about romantic relationships as isolating. We all have that one friend who disappears the moment they meet a new love interest. But looking at partnership as a way to expand, instead of contract our social circle can make it even more fulfilling—even if you initially get nervous around new people.

This raises the uncomfortable question: How much should we consider other people's opinions of our potential partner when selecting a spouse? After all, they (presumably) know us well and might be able to see things we can't. In many cases, the answer might depend on one's cultural context. In some cultures, family approval is imperative, while in others, families might be more hands-off or uninvolved, making it less clear how much you should let their two cents affect your partner selection.

If you fall into the second camp, it can be hard to even get honest feedback from loved ones about your partner. Many people don't want to overstep, or they avoid sharing their true feelings so as not to make things awkward or contentious. It's obviously worth considering if the people closest to you have a history of only revealing their true feelings *after* you break up. If that's the case, it's probably smart to actively open the door for an honest discussion, emphasizing how valuable their input is. I certainly wish

I had done this more while dating certain people instead of just insisting, "He's way more talkative when we're alone!" or "You don't *really* know him!" over and over again. As an outgoing (and loud) person, finally having a partner who is just as gregarious as me—and more importantly, whose strengths were just simply apparent and didn't need to constantly be explained or reassured to others—has made a world of difference that I didn't know I was missing before.

An important caveat of inviting feedback is, of course, whether that friend or relative has a habit of automatically hating every person you've ever dated. You also only want to ask people you know have your best intentions in mind. If they do share something negative, it's fair to take some time to digest the feedback. As Jessica says, "their judgment shouldn't be our judgment, but we should be open to being curious about how our partner is perceived through the eyes of the people who are most important to us." Even if it takes multiple meetings for everyone to really get to know each other.

Finding that balance between prioritizing what we want and accepting outside feedback is a difficult line to walk, and it can take some trial and error. Like that time my mom told me when I was 23 that I didn't *have* to move in with my boyfriend at the time just so I could have a nicer apartment, and I ignored her—only to break up pretty much immediately after signing the lease. In my defense, it's hard to listen to your mom's opinion about relationships when you're 23 (and when you really want a dishwasher). But now that I'm older I take her opinion far more seriously. And when she told me that John seemed like someone who would encourage me to have a "big life," I knew to believe her, and it made me more confident in my decision to marry him.

As a first-generation American, Huma has often felt stuck between two cultures. While she wouldn't call her parents devout or even conservative, they are still practicing Muslims who had an arranged marriage in Pakistan. In fact, pretty much all of the elders in her family had arranged marriages. This tradition combined with growing up in the States made her feel conflicted about what romantic relationships "should" look and feel like. She loved rom-coms but knew that the Western version of dating was out of the question. So instead of having to keep that part of her life secret from her parents, she focused on school and friends and avoided romance until well into her twenties. Her mom put some pressure on her to have an arranged marriage after she graduated from college, but Huma resisted. Despite her own parents' history and the external voices around her, deep down she knew she was meant to find her person on her own.

When Huma finally met that person at age 27 through her job at a college campus, she didn't go into the relationship having a glorified view of marriage. She actually had a bit of a tarnished one. Huma shared, "When I thought about marriage, what first came to mind wasn't all the things I wanted. It was all the things I didn't want." She'd seen so many women she knew sacrifice themselves for their husbands. She didn't want to follow in their footsteps.

That's partly why she was so drawn to the kindness of her now-husband, Reza. After hearing so many stories of unkind men growing up, Huma could sense Reza was different. So even though he was an Iranian immigrant from a Shia family and Huma is a first-generation Pakistani American from a Sunni family, she took the leap and they began dating. In secret! Huma knew she couldn't introduce Reza to her parents unless she was sure they were going to get married. So even though Huma was still living at home, which made logistics rather tricky, she managed to get to know Reza on her own terms. One night, seven months into their courtship, they both decided they were ready to commit. Reza finally came to meet her family and shortly after that they were officially engaged.

At first glance, this might not seem like a story of rebellion. A Muslim woman married the first Muslim man she ever dated after getting her parents' approval. Her surprising autonomy is only found in the details. Although Reza is Muslim, he isn't the same sect as Huma and comes from a West Asian country whereas she is from a South Asian one. Huma met him on her own through work and kept their relationship private until she was ready to include her family. And, after getting married, she continued to forgo tradition by moving out of her parents' home and not having children right away. Instead of simply accepting every single expectation that her loved ones had for her partner selection, Huma was actively breaking generational patterns of behavior that didn't sit right with her and creating a new timeline and process for herself.

In Huma's words, "I feel like until I got married, I lived so much for my family, for the perception and trying to really fit this mold of being a good daughter. I really lived for other things more than myself. So I didn't feel like I was finally an adult, like an independent adult, living for myself until I got married." And picking Reza as her husband, instead of a more conservative spouse, was a large part of what made that possible. Her family's opinion of her husband still mattered. But her opinion, which was one Huma formed in private, came first.

So many couples' stories "break the rules" in terms of finding a suitable partner. People find each other young or without much forethought. Others had everything stacked against them and still fell in love. And some—and by some, I mean me—defied their own partner checklist in the hopes that things might work out anyway. But no matter how you choose who you choose, it's still undeniable that much of the real work is done *after* you pick your person.

It's easy to fall into a trap of thinking that if we just pick right from the start, then everything will be okay. I was certainly guilty of this. After my broken engagement, I felt extra pressure not to choose "wrong" again. I thought being strategic from the beginning would protect me from more heartbreak. But Dr. Shelly is right to point out that when we retroactively blame our role in the partner selection for things not working out, "It's a way to kind of reclaim control, because if it is me, then there is something that I can do that will make a difference. The alternative, which is to accept that shit happens to us that is out of our control, is actually really scary."

In a weird way, accepting this lack of control instead of rejecting it can help you gain your confidence back after heartbreak. Sure, sometimes we don't put enough thought into who we give our heart to, or we actively ignore obvious incompatibilities. But a lot of the time, we did make an educated bet on another person. We just forget the part that it's still a bet. No matter how good the odds are.

With that in mind, here are some more (fun?) questions to explore:

QUESTIONS TO ASK YOURSELF

- Is my idea of who my partner "should" be overly rigid?
- Am I consciously or subconsciously not as open to partners with certain demographic differences from me (e.g., financial, educational, religious, etc.)? If so, what is my reasoning?
- Has my romantic history taught me anything significant about who I am or am not compatible with?
- What do I bring to the table as a partner? Is there anything I want to improve?
- Would I mind if my partner and I had separate hobbies? Why or why not?

- Why do I think the prominent couples in my life work well together or, possibly, don't work well together?

QUESTIONS TO DISCUSS WITH YOUR PARTNER

- In what ways am I how you envisioned your future spouse? In what ways am I not?
- What makes you think I will be a good life partner and not just a good boyfriend/girlfriend/themfriend?
- Are we incompatible in any ways? If so, does it bother or worry you?
- Out of everyone on the planet, why did you pick me?

Finding a compatible partner can take a lot of time, effort, and heartbreak. But once you find that person... you still have a lot of work to do, which is why this book isn't over yet.

3

WILL YOU BE MY... ROOMMATE?

Why Get Married When You Could Just Cohabit

Not too long ago, I was introduced to the term "Boston Marriage." It's a phrase that was used to describe cohabitation between two financially independent women in the nineteenth and twentieth centuries who happened to live together and share domestic chores.

If you are reading this with your eyebrows raised, you aren't alone. While at the time most of society assumed these were platonic partnerships, it's likely that many of the women were also romantically involved, and the only difference between their relationships and a legal marriage was the legal part. This gets at one of the biggest questions regarding modern marriage: Is it really any different than just living together?

As someone who has lived with three men and successfully married only one of them, I would say yes. But I am also a person who attaches a lot of symbolic meaning to marriage. I feel more at peace and connected to John now that we're married. (Partly due to the fact that I spent the first nine months of our cohabitation annoyed that he hadn't proposed yet. Even after we picked out the ring together and I knew it was sitting somewhere in the house calling to me like I was Gollum.) But what about more normal, rational people who haven't been obsessed with getting married since they were a small child? Does it make that much of a difference to them?

Now that our culture has shifted and most people are no longer shocked to find out two consenting adults are sharing a bed without a marriage license, are we unnecessarily complicating things by still getting married? And aside from getting to plan a wedding and post a lot of perfectly lit engagement photos, are there really any long-lasting impacts that separate cohabiting life partners from spouses? Could living together without getting married be a perfect workaround for younger generations who desire partnership but dislike the traditionalizing effects of marriage?

It turns out Arielle Kuperberg, the sociologist I spoke to in Chapter One, was asking a lot of those same questions herself. She set out to "prove that marriage doesn't make any difference" through her research only to realize…it does. Arielle simply couldn't ignore the legal and financial benefits. Marriage, for example, "gives people the legal protection to be a stay-at-home parent," which is a rather big difference that can significantly shape what kind of parenting lifestyle you can have.

But more surprising than the legal differences, marriage also appears to genuinely change people's behavior and expectations for each other. For example, Arielle's research suggests that "you're more likely to help your partner pay for college if they want to go back to school if you're married versus somebody you're living with." It seems that marriage, something one could easily dismiss as a piece of paper and a new relationship title, can actually ignite emotional and practical changes in the way partners treat each other and the bets and risks they are willing to make together. While I myself couldn't find hard proof, I suspect this kind of behavior extends to other things like paying off your partner's debt or investing in their small business. The motivation behind these behaviors might be that married couples tend to view themselves as part of a single unit, where one person's gain is a win for the team.

This combination of legal and symbolic differences around marriage also makes it much harder and more expensive for people to end their relationships. And while some of us might view that as negative, Arielle points out that marriage, unlike cohabitation, cultivates what she refers to as "enforceable trust." This means that, in addition to trusting each other interpersonally, the government can also "step in and enforce how much you trust each other because you've got legal paperwork." There is an extra liability baked in, so it can feel psychologically safer to financially invest in or with the other person because they can't just up and leave you without consequences. This manifests in the legal rewards too: you can buy a house together without needing to get lawyers involved to protect yourself, and you don't have to pay inheritance tax if your spouse dies.

In 2019, the *Washington Post* provocatively boasted about the importance of marriage by publishing an article titled, "Married people have happier, healthier relationships than unmarried couples who live together, data show." The subheading that got to the heart of the differences unpacked in the article stated: "Cohabitating couples are more likely to cite practical reasons, such as finances, for their relationship status, while married pairs are more motivated by love and children." This is a rather big (and inflammatory) claim! Is there something to the idea that cohabiting couples' living arrangements often comes down to money and pragmatism ("might as well save time on my commute") while married couples actually want to build a life together?

At first glance, it does seem like marriage continually produces more satisfied and committed couples than cohabitation does. Although, again, this might be due to the research from Chapter One that married people tend to be wealthier and happier already. Or that being married provides you with a level of social acceptance and rewards that positively influences your overall well-being. Or maybe there is just some deep-rooted psychological shift that lets people mentally and emotionally depend on their partners more once they become spouses. I'm sure for most people, it's a mix of all three.

But to play devil's advocate to this article: while I'm sure the data set technically supported this headline, it feels like we are painting with too wide of a brush. Especially when we return to the idea that in many ways, marriage has become a financially unattainable class symbol. Isn't it possible that cohabitating couples listed financial reasons for moving in together over love because we live in a society with exorbitant rent prices and underpaying jobs? And that for many Americans, monetary concerns would top the list as an explanation for most of their behaviors?

I don't think moving in together primarily to save money means you are doomed. But I do think it might rush couples to take a big emotional step that they wouldn't feel as pressured to make if they were more financially comfortable. Would fewer people cohabit as early in their relationships if everyone could afford to live on their own?

While the percentage of unmarried couples living together has been growing for decades, the COVID-19 pandemic certainly increased the rate of cohabitation, especially among younger people. *Bloomberg* reported in March 2023 that around 650,000 more unmarried 18- to

25-year-olds lived with their partners than before 2020. The desire to save money seemed to be the driving factor. This is worrying to me on a societal level—people shouldn't be making huge relationship decisions because of wage inequality and high rent prices. Rushing into cohabitation might not be the right emotional choice for all partners even if it's the right practical one.

Of course, not all couples are looking to stay together for the rest of their lives. One huge advantage to the rise and normalization of cohabitating partners is that it simply isn't that big of a deal if you live with someone, break up and then live with someone else and break up. If things don't work out, there's less legal entanglements to wade through. While it is no doubt emotionally taxing, this type of relationship history doesn't leave a person with a scarlet letter the way it would have in the past. Plus, it is fun to live with a partner—even if it doesn't last forever. It eliminates the need to constantly pack an overnight bag and, in my case, means I don't have to walk the dogs at night by myself anymore. You're in the mood to hang out with your favorite person? Great news! They're already in the living room.

When broadly comparing living together versus getting married, I think it's important to keep in mind that people cohabit for various reasons. Sure, some do it for money or convenience. Some do it as a sort of trial period before getting married. While others might not have enough money to get married and/or don't want to be on the hook for their partner's finances. Plenty of people might also view it as a way to become life partners—without involving the government. For all my fondness of marriage licenses, there is something beautiful to be said about committing to someone day after day even though no one is saying you have to. It's the sentiment, *I don't need a piece of paper to tell me who to love.*

Regardless of one's reasoning, I think we can all agree that what matters most is that both partners are on the same page about what it means to live together, since it is naturally a less defined commitment than marriage. Is this arrangement a first step or placeholder until an inevitable marriage? Or is cohabitation our end goal? Are we going to join finances or just split things 50/50? What do we call each other? You don't want to go through all the hassle of moving only to find out you have different answers to those questions.

With society's growing acceptance of unwed couples living together, I think we might be at a turning point when it comes to the (constant) debate of cohabiting versus marriage. If the current trend continues and more and more people cohabit without getting married, it's possible marriage's legal *and* symbolic advantages will start to fade. If, in thirty years, Gen Z, Gen Alpha and federal law no longer draw such a stark line between matrimony and cohabitation, the societal rewards for being married might decrease or disappear altogether. (Especially if the current draconian health care system starts to change and everyone has their own benefits.) Things take a while to become truly normalized, and we might still be in the middle of a seismic shift wherein cohabitation becomes the standard—and maybe only religious people or old-school romantics bother with matrimony in the future. I wouldn't necessarily put all my money on it, given the strong emotional attachment so many of us have to marriage. But then again, I'm a millennial who still wears skin tight pants. I'm not exactly on the forefront of change.

There's no one-size-fits-all for every relationship situation, and one type of arrangement is not always better or worse. But here are some conversation starters that might help you figure out what feels right for you:

QUESTIONS TO ASK YOURSELF

- Is there a difference to me between living with someone and marrying someone? Why do I feel that way?
- Is my connection and level of dependence with my partner influenced by the framework (married or cohabiting) of our relationship? Why or why not?
- Would I be disappointed if I lived with my partner but never married them? Why or why not?

QUESTIONS TO DISCUSS WITH YOUR PARTNER

- What are/were our reasons for moving in together?
- How did/do you know when you are ready to live with a partner? What are the signs?

- If we marry, will our relationship feel different? (Or, does our relationship feel different now that we are married?)

As we head into our next chapter, I just want to give a quick reminder that research studies and surveys simply shed insight on the *majority* of people. That still leaves a large percentage who go against the grain, and are perfectly happy doing so. Like all those married celebrities who still live in separate mansions.

4
FOREVER (UNCERTAIN)

The Modern Epidemic of Commitment Phobia

As someone who has always had a (unhealthy) fixation on partnership, I'll admit I've struggled to understand other people's fear of commitment. Why wouldn't you want a best romantic friend who has told the entire world that you are also their best romantic friend? Growing up, it seemed like a surefire way to alleviate all my fears that I was unlovable and meant to die alone.

But beyond the biases of my own experience, I've come to realize that constantly being uncertain if you should move forward with someone, for whatever reason, is exhausting. And not just for the person experiencing that endless questioning, but also for their partner. If a couple finds themselves in a mental dance of commitment issues from one partner (or both partners), is it possible to somehow not take it personally and/or let it destroy your relationship? Or is this type of uncertainty always a clear sign that you aren't right for each other?

I've also started to wonder if problems with commitment have shifted in recent years from being an individual issue to a generational struggle. The Pew Research Center has found that millennials are less likely to get married than past generations, and when they do get married, they tend to tie the knot later in life. And I strongly suspect this trend will continue for Gen Z. While I refuse to theorize about one single reason for this shift, I do think some larger social forces have contributed to younger generations' reluctance to pick one long-term partner early on. Beyond the increased partner options and the diminishing social pressure to wed young, millennials also grew up with a lot of divorce happening among the baby boomer generation, which has likely made them more hesitant to dive into marriage. Not to mention the world has changed, with what seems like a constant uptick in financial and global instability impacting many areas of younger generations' lives. It's no wonder commitment doesn't come so easily anymore, whether it comes to relationships, jobs or homeowning.

But just because something is hard doesn't mean it's impossible. And given that many younger people still desire partnership and/or marriage, it feels important to explore how to potentially work through these commitment issues and better understand the real reason behind their doubts. To help us navigate all this, I enlisted Elizabeth Earnshaw and Sara Vicendese, two therapists who are well-versed in how draining it can feel to constantly wonder, *am I making a huge mistake?*

Many of you are probably familiar with Attachment Theory. One of its basic premises is that our relationships with our early caregivers shape our relationships later in life. As Elizabeth explains, "When we're growing up, we have lots of experiences that tell us whether or not relationships are safe... And if we learned that whenever we seek a secure bond, there isn't security there, then what starts to happen is we become wired with what's called insecure attachment. We feel this sense of, 'connection isn't safe for me,'" which then generates anxiety about connection.

This usually has two possible outcomes. The first is a more overt, frenetic type of anxiety. The second is that the person tends to shut down and becomes avoidant. Those who are anxiously attached are often called pursuers. And those who are avoidantly attached are known in the mental health biz as withdrawers. And they very often end up in relationships with each other, which is fun for everyone. (Including the couples therapists who are paid to help them navigate this dynamite dynamic.)

As a formerly anxiously attached person, despite having stable caregivers, I know what it's like for connection to be a source of stress. I used to live in near constant fear that my boyfriends didn't love me enough or love me at all. This would then lead me to behaviors that often stifled and sabotaged my relationships. (Which is a story for another book—that I already wrote if you want to check it out!)

For a long time, it was impossible for me to view avoidant behavior as anything other than a personal affront and proof that my suspicions of being unloved were right. If someone wasn't over the moon to commit to me immediately (or on my preordained timeline), they must not love me in the *right* way, which meant they didn't love me enough and would inevitably leave me. But through learning more about attachment and navigating my current relationship, I've been able to dismantle my misconceptions and have more empathy and understanding for people wired differently than me.

While I have always viewed commitment as a safe haven from loneliness, many other people view commitment as intrinsically scary. For some, like my husband, the fear comes from the threat of potentially getting hurt. They don't want to commit until they reach a certain level of trust and time with their partner. And given that trust and time, the fear starts to dissipate.

For others who resist commitment, the reason is more complex. While combining lives with another person always involves a variety of risks (including the possibility your partner might eat your leftovers without asking), for some people the threat is that they might lose themselves in the relationship, and even more so in marriage.

Elizabeth explains, "When you want to commit with

somebody, you have to hold both independence and dependence in the same body. You have to be able to say, 'I can still be myself, and I can still be with you.'" It's that adage that two things can be true at once. But for a lot of people, they think that they can only pick one. Or, even if they don't think this overtly, they can start to act according to the subconscious assumption that the options are either: be your full, independent self, or be in a committed relationship. They can either continue to pursue music in their free time as a single person or spend *every* weekend with their partner's annoying family and never have time to play guitar again. And when the options are framed in that way, it's easy to see why marriage isn't always an enticing choice because with the gain of partnership comes the loss of who you are and what you love.

The challenge then becomes learning how to hold on to both things, even if you grew up thinking that dichotomy isn't possible. As Elizabeth explains, it's about choosing to remain close to someone even when you want to run away. And for those who are more anxiously attached and feel untethered without constant closeness, it's learning to give your partner space even when what you really want to do is chase. Or text five times in a row.

But how important is it to know *why* we pull away or overly pursue versus simply identifying our patterns and working to change them? While Elizabeth doesn't think it's necessary to do a yearslong deep dive into your childhood or early caregiver relationships, she does believe that "it can be helpful for us to have a coherent narrative of why we are who we are... It feels less chaotic." Uncertainty in relationships might be a given, but chaos doesn't have to be. And self-awareness also makes it easier to offer yourself self-compassion.

For example, maybe jealousy isn't an inherent part of a person's personality, but a result of having been cheated on by an ex for many years. It can be useful to the individual and their partner when they're able to say something like, "I know I pull away when things get tough, but I grew up watching my dad do the same thing." Or, "When you don't call me back, it stirs up some of my past abandonment issues so I have an exaggerated reaction." This type of explanation helps those behaviors feel less like a personal attack on the partner. And hopefully, after figuring out a bit of the why, the way those partners interact in relationships can change over time. None of us have to remain stuck in our patterns or the patterns of our caregivers.

As Elizabeth beautifully said, "change takes time, but effort doesn't." You can make the decision to put in the effort to change at any moment. Even this one.

Or this one.

All this being said, anxiety is an equal-opportunity offender, and there are some people who feel commitment reticence about their specific partner even if they don't have an insecure attachment style. And this uncertainty often becomes amplified under pressures of commitment. So when marriage is introduced to the conversation, it can become hard to decipher if your anxiety is logical and fact-based, or if it is just getting in the way of your happiness.

If someone finds themselves in this type of predicament, Elizabeth says it can be beneficial to ask yourself, "Is this a pattern in my life? Or is it just with this person?" If the answer is the latter, the question then becomes, "Is it a pattern with this person or is it just in this moment?" Because, as Elizabeth deftly points out, "We're not going to feel perfect with our partner all the time. And if we seek that, that's seeking perfection." (Which I've heard from many reliable sources is sadly unattainable.)

However, if someone realizes they're experiencing this type of questioning in *every* relationship, they'll probably need to realize that they can't fix the problem simply by "partner hopping." If uncertainty has been a common theme with all the people you've ever been with, is there a deeper root to what's going on? Do you have unrealistic expectations? Are you always worried that you are "missing out" on someone better? Do you keep dating people with clear red flags, so you don't have to get too serious? If those tendencies don't change, it's unlikely a new partner will trigger different feelings—even if they are very sparkly and exciting at first.

On the flip side, if you've consistently felt anxious about your choice of partner from the beginning, and that's *not* something you normally experience in a relationship, Elizabeth says it's possible that "your anxiety is actually telling you the other person is a mismatch." Sometimes this worry boils down to issues that can be effectively worked out with time, patience, and couples therapy, like having different communication styles. Other times, though, you might realize the issue isn't going to go anywhere and you have to decide how you feel about that, which is where discernment therapy can come into play. Discernment therapy is meant to help someone determine if they actually want to stay or leave *before* diving into the hard work involved in traditional couples therapy. It also gives that person support if they make the decision to walk away, which can otherwise feel extreme and unmanageable on their own. Plus it's a lot less sensational and public than going on a show like Netflix's *The Ultimatum* to figure out if you should or shouldn't get married.

Sometimes, though, what appears to be "commitment issues" might be better described as two people having different commitment *speeds* or *routes*. This was certainly the case in my own relationship, which caused a mild to moderate amount of tension. For me, getting to a place where I felt ready to cohabitate was the tricky part. I had to ask myself, was I willing—so soon after a major heartbreak—to uproot my home for another person without any guarantee it would work out? I ultimately decided the answer was yes, because I am either brave or foolish. (I prefer the brave framing, but check back in with me in a few decades.) After twelvish months of dating, I felt ready to leave my apartment of over seven years so we could live together in a new place. Once I took that leap of faith, engagement felt like the obvious next step. I had gotten through the scariest part, and now it was time to get a pretty ring and plan a big party.

But John didn't see it that way. To him, agreeing to move in wasn't the same thing as agreeing to immediately marry each other, because our roads to commitment were different. He wanted time to live together and enjoy a new phase of our relationship. He also didn't want to "rush into anything" because his commitment speed was a lot slower than mine. I had to learn to accept that the idea of getting engaged after only a year, despite being in our thirties, bumped up against his notion of how successful relationships work. While for me, *not* getting engaged after being together for a year following my broken engagement bumped up against my trauma of my partner not being sure about me.

In another version of our relationship, these conflicting commitment routes might have led to disaster. I could have let my insecurity demand we get engaged before he was ready. And he could have staunchly refused, causing us to break up. But instead we were able to have some pretty frank discussions about *why* we had different speeds so we could understand each other better and come to a place of compromise. I wanted to *decrease* the amount of time before marriage to appease my anxiety and have tangible proof that he loved me, and he wanted to *increase* the time before marriage to protect himself and make sure he wouldn't get hurt. We both had the same goal: married and happy. Our baggage just demanded different paths to get there, and once we understood that, we were able to meet in the middle.

I was pleased to hear that therapist Sara Vicendese agreed that curiosity, and not resentment, is the way to go if partners disagree on when or how to commit. She says that if a couple walked through her door and only one of them wanted to get married, "I'd be very curious why marriage was so important to one partner and equally curious why it wasn't for the other." And once those reasons are expressed, the question becomes, "Can they understand where their partner is coming from? Do they think it's valid?"

I love that she uses the term valid, because it is one thing to know how your partner feels, and another to view their feelings as holding as much merit as your own. Especially when your own feelings conflict with it. It is a skill and not a given to be able to support another person's emotions even when you don't agree with their logic or reasoning. (One that I learned rather far into adulthood and only with the help of a master's degree in psychology.)

But of course, it's important to remember that commitment to a relationship isn't exclusively tied to marriage for everyone, and not wanting to marry your partner doesn't inherently mean you feel uncertain about them. As Sara points out, some couples have a "philosophical difference of opinion on marriage"—and that is categorically different than not being sure about committing to a specific partner. If one partner has said something along the lines of, "I don't believe in the institution of marriage. I think it's archaic. It doesn't align with my values. But I will be here every single day. I want to have a family with you and I love you,"—and their actions also align with this—it seems like a strong signal to not equate their reluctance to marry with a reluctance to wanting to commit to your relationship. Even if your anxious attachment style is SCREAMING that you must be unlovable or disgusting if they don't want to race down to the courthouse and legally proclaim their devotion.

If one partner's path toward commitment involves marriage and the other's doesn't, it becomes a different kind of discussion focused on flexibility. Is the pro-marriage partner able to find a way to feel safe and secure in their partnership without being legally wed and having their commitment be socially recognized? Or is the anti-marriage partner able to get to a place where they can create their own version of marriage and not feel like they're participating in an institution they don't align with? For the sake of love and the avoidance of all those nasty breakup posts, I hope so. But if neither person is willing to budge, then it seems pretty unlikely that a shared future is possible or, even more importantly, enjoyable.

At a certain point, discussions can only take you so far and a decision must be made. As Sara put it, "Owning your relationship needs is critical. If you know you want to get married and your partner doesn't, you shouldn't stay quiet about that." And neither should your partner. Neither of you can just hope the other will change their mind. There needs to be some form of flexibility, or you both need to move on. And in some cases, there might even be a (healthy) ultimatum. For me, that took the form of a verbal agreement that John and I would be engaged within the year of moving in or I would leave, because marriage is a priority for me. Thankfully, he got that proposal in right under the wire. (And with perfect execution I might add.)

Operating on two different commitment speeds doesn't automatically doom a relationship so long as you're willing to have some pretty frank discussions. But sometimes doing that is easier said than done. When Zoe met Will during their first year of college, she didn't think she'd one day be in therapy making a plan to leave if Will didn't propose by summer 2020. In fact, Zoe had gone out of her way to avoid this outcome by clearly stating her intention to one day get married and have a family when they started their relationship—even though she was only 21 and Will was 18 at the time. But after years of being together and cohabiting, Zoe wasn't any closer to getting engaged, and Will had a habit of avoiding the topic all together.

So when Zoe's therapist proposed that Zoe create a timeline for herself, she agreed. She would leave Will if he didn't propose by the summer. The tricky part of this ultimatum? She didn't plan to tell Will about it. Zoe wanted Will to propose because he wanted to marry her, not because he had been pressured into it. For Zoe, getting married symbolized a lot of things that wouldn't feel the same if the proposal came about only as a reaction instead of a genuine want. In an ideal world, Will would come to recognize what he had in front of him before the calendar hit June, or else Zoe would have to walk out the door to uphold her agreement with herself.

None of that happened. Instead, Zoe's secret ultimatum came to light during a fight, and Will didn't end up proposing until after the deadline in the fall. But it was through learning about Zoe's timeline that Will was finally forced to confront his own feelings about marriage, which wasn't easy. Will explained, "I grew up in like, a pretty emotionally repressed kind of situation. I wasn't really taught and didn't really understand how to deal with my own emotions or really know how to identify how I'm feeling. And that's something that definitely made the whole engagement thing kind of complicated for me."

There was a lot to work through, and while Will did eventually propose, this decision didn't solve all their issues. Instead, the worst time in their relationship actually came *after* they were finally engaged. It seemed that, despite's Zoe's hopes, committing to marriage didn't lead Will to be more committed to their day-to-day relationship. Zoe had finally reached her goal only to find her partnership in its most dire state yet. She was plagued with fears that Will only proposed because he was worried he was going to lose her if he didn't. And that isn't the same thing as two people being excited to marry each other.

Zoe suspects that part of the problem was that once Will had ticked off the box of proposing, he didn't feel like he needed to pay as much attention to her or put in any effort. Will owned up to not being considerate during that time, and he even admitted that when Zoe would stand up for herself, it would make him feel bad, and then he'd react by getting angry. He cared more about how Zoe's feelings made him feel about himself than what her feelings actually meant.

So how did they get from that place to the happy couple sitting on a Zoom call genuinely looking forward to their wedding in a few weeks? Part of it was Will taking an active role in changing his behavior. But another huge part was them finally clearing up some misunderstandings they had about what marriage meant to each of them. For Zoe, her desire to get married wasn't tied to any legal or financial benefits since common law relationships in Canada have all the same rights as marriages. Instead, it came down to a feeling of being chosen and holding a special place in the other person's life. And for Will, marriage meant kids. And he wasn't ready to have kids.

It's funny how you can know someone so deeply and yet not realize they misunderstand your beliefs around marriage and what it signifies to you. Yes, Zoe wants kids. But she doesn't need them right away. But Will privately believed that getting married equated starting a family, which explained a lot of his hesitation. Once this misunderstanding finally came to light, Zoe was able to calm fears she didn't previously know Will was experiencing. And he was able to let go of the worry that marriage would immediately and fundamentally change his relationship and everyday life. Through all these open conversations, Will finally got to a place where he was sincerely excited to marry Zoe. Then, something surprising—or maybe unsurprising—happened. Once Zoe heard him say he wanted to marry her for his own sake, she realized she didn't actually need to get married anymore because he had already made her feel chosen and committed.

But even if Zoe no longer needed to get married following their two-year engagement, she still wanted a wedding. She wanted to party. And when we signed off our interview, I was excited for her to finally live out her bridal fantasy. That's why my heart sank when I opened an email from her a few weeks later that said, "I got Covid the night before the wedding and it blew up all our plans." I braced myself to read that her day had been brutally ruined. But, in a twist made for a rom-com, that's not what happened at all. While Zoe was a wreck the night before, Will stepped in to make the necessary changes to make it all still happen. They ended up getting married on a raised balcony in his parents' backyard with enough distance between them and their guests to keep everyone safe and for Zoe to feel like a literal queen. And Will's determination to marry her "no matter what" extinguished any lingering fears she had that he was just getting married to make her happy.

The day also gave her some clarity. Will outwardly showing his commitment to their friends and family, even if it was from a balcony while infected with Covid, was more important to Zoe than signing the marriage license.

She wrapped up the email to me by saying that after eight years of being together, she doesn't feel much different being married. But Will does. Even if he couldn't explain why.

We all have moments in our lives that fundamentally change how we see the world: learning that the Sahara Desert used to be a rainforest, finding out that your buttoned-up grandma loves to smoke weed in secret, realizing it tastes better to heat up old pizza in a toaster oven instead of a microwave. For me, my entire perspective changed the night my ex-fiancé left. Any sense of certainty I had about my life walked out the door with the man I once was so sure was going to be my husband. It made me realize, perhaps belatedly, that anything can happen to you at any moment, which is not a great reveal for someone with an anxiety disorder. The thing about the human brain (or at least my version of it) is that it craves certainty and control. And my experience with my ex taught me that choosing to build your life with another person robs you of both.

That's why it's ironic that we are often raised to think of marriage as a "safe" choice, when in reality we have no idea what's going to happen in the future. I did all my "homework" when it came to my ex. I knew his family. I knew his friends. I knew far too much about his confusing job in "customer success." I was certain that my decision to marry him was a smart one because I was certain that it would last. But I can't force anyone to love me forever or prevent them from changing with time. All I can do is work on my personal relationship with uncertainty, which is far easier said than done. It's pretty difficult to confidently make a lifelong commitment when you have no idea where that life will lead you or your partner and how it will change you both.

One big revelation before my wedding was realizing that I wasn't afraid to marry the *current* version of John. I like this version of him. I know this version. But what if he dramatically changes? What if I do? Do we have to stay together simply because earlier versions of ourselves signed a legal contract and publicly cut an ice cream cake? (You read that right! We had an ice cream cake at the wedding.)

During my conversation with Sara, we were discussing "intention" and I was trying to make the point that what's important is for your *intention* to be until death— even if that doesn't end up happening. She gently replied, "I would never hold anyone accountable for knowing how they're going to feel in the future. It's unfair and unrealistic."

When I read these words now, I absolutely agree. However, at the time of our conversation, I could only view what she was saying in relation to my own trauma. I felt like my ex-fiancé didn't even attempt to fix things—he just walked out without giving us any time to work on our relationship. I didn't want anyone to give my ex-fiancé an out for what I saw as unnecessarily hurtful behavior. So I quipped back, "But don't you think that once you've made that commitment, that even if your feelings change, that you have an obligation to at least *try* to work on things?"

Then she hit me with the kind of response that makes you rethink your entire approach to life. She asked me if I view marriage as an obligation. She said, "We all hope that our partners will care enough to do the work when hard times come, to be willing to fight for the relationship... But I don't like the term 'obligation.' I prefer 'choice.'" I know you shouldn't ever feel "owned" by a therapist, but, oh man, did she win that conversation. I can barely predict how I am going to feel in five minutes let alone in fifty years. Expecting someone to maintain a feeling forever is not only unrealistic, but unkind. And your initial intention, however lovely, doesn't really matter if you start to view marriage as a continuous choice instead of a prison. We have to give ourselves—and our partners, the people we love most in the world—the freedom to change and grow. Even if they grow away from us.

Sara, through what I can only refer to as a master class in reframing, helped me realize I don't like the term "obligation" either. It implies you could be behaving in a way disingenuous to your own wants in order to satisfy something outside of yourself. And, look, sometimes love does involve doing things we don't really want to do. Who among us actually enjoys *all* of our partner's interests, or delights in applying topical medication to a loved one's hard to reach places? Not me! But I think there is a difference between doing those things out of love and commitment versus a feeling of obligation. When you act out of love or commitment, that is honoring something that matters to you instead of being motivated by societal messages regarding how you should behave as a spouse. Even if you aren't in the mood to show up in the moment, you know this person is a priority in your life and you're going to act as such.

This may all seem like semantics, but I would rather my partner try to work through things with me because our marriage is important to them, rather than stay purely due to a heavy sense of obligation to "do the right thing." It's the difference between, *I want to stay married* and *I should stay married*. I want to be someone's active choice, not their burden. And if they no longer want to choose me, for whatever reason, I have to be okay letting them go. And at the end of the day, everyone has different thresholds for how long they are willing to work on their problems and different criteria for what type of marriage is or isn't worth continuing.

I think the hardest thing about being afraid that your spouse will one day change is that no good therapist will tell you those fears are unfounded. Both partners in a relationship are going to change over time. The hope, Sara says, is that you will "celebrate those changes." But if those changes lead one or both of you to wanting "out" of the marriage, maybe that is not an inherent betrayal. (Despite my former misguided mindset.)

Deciding to stay together "no matter what" isn't always an adaptive concept when you have no way of knowing what that *what* is or who you'll even be when the *what* happens. It also robs you of personal agency. As Sara points out, that approach puts you in the less empowering, re-signed mindset of, "Well, I'm here. I guess there is nothing I can do about it if there's a problem." That's not the attitude I take when it comes to any other aspect of my life. Why should I become completely passive just because I'm married and we're both miserable? I've started to come around to the idea that aside from the decision to have a child, all commitments—from your career to your sexuality to your location to your religion—are allowed to be revised as needed. Parenthood, at least to me, remains the only lifelong arrangement where once you're a parent, you stay a parent. (In whatever form that takes.) Others might feel the same rules apply when you become a spouse, and it's not my place to push against that. But I will say divorce has been normalized for a reason.

Elizabeth agrees that when entering into a marriage, "It needs to be more a commitment to honesty, more a commitment to the willingness to have conversations, the willingness to be a good partner, than to be completely committed to having something work, even if it's hor-rendous."

This raises the eternal question of, why bother to get married if you're leaving room for the possibility that it will end? I think one answer comes down to fear and how much power you're willing to give it. Yes, marriage is filled with uncertainty. You cannot entirely control what will happen in your life or your relationship. But is that a good enough reason to not even get in the ring and fight? Sara treats many people who "aren't fully engaging in their lives because they are afraid of a painful outcome." She says, "If we take risks, we win some and lose some. Without risk, we lose out on everything."

Seeing it put this bluntly, it's easier for me to recognize that I don't want to be someone who refuses to fully engage. I don't want a life of no outcomes because I'm always avoiding the bad ones. I want to take the risk and put trust in my future self to manage whatever comes her way. Because, as I'm slowly learning, the bad doesn't always diminish the good. And if we want any shot at the good stuff, we have to risk letting other people get close enough to hurt us.

Some people's relationship journeys hurt more than others, with twists and turns no one could predict. Nina was a late bloomer when it came to dating. She wasn't into hook-up culture or interested in something super serious and those seemed to be the only options at her college. So she focused on other areas of her life, including a graduate degree, and didn't find herself in her first relationship until she was 27 when she met Trevor on a dating app. They dated for a few months before he called it off because he wasn't satisfied with the relationship. He then reappeared a few months later and seemed to be in a better place. They got back together, dated for a few more years, and decided to get married. That's when things abruptly changed.

After they got married, it felt like a switch flipped in

him. He was suddenly saying horrible things to her he had never expressed before. Things like "if only you'd lose a bunch of weight, then you'd be the wife I wanted" and "you should dress in clothes that only please me." This was not a man she had married in haste. This was someone she had been with for *five* years. Yet, the emotional abuse only started once they were husband and wife.

His sudden change was disorienting and painful. Nina desperately tried to figure out what had sparked this ugly transformation. At one point he told her, "I've never loved you. This marriage was all a lie." And yet, he didn't want to get divorced. He would fluctuate between saying things that should never be said out loud and declaring he wanted to work on their relationship with couples therapy. But Nina knew she deserved better than this flip-flopping and abuse, so just six months after getting married she insisted on separating.

Getting divorced so quickly after getting married shattered her self-concept. As she explained, "I am a 'good' girl who made good decisions. And so suddenly being the person who was getting divorced six months after she got married was very at odds with the way that I thought about myself and who I was." It didn't matter that Trevor was the one who changed and she couldn't possibly have seen that coming.

Luckily, Nina didn't let this horrible experience cause her to give up on love. In fact, she did the opposite, and forced herself to get back out there before her walls went all the way up and got stuck in place. For a while, none of the men she was meeting really ignited anything in her.

Then she met Dan. Dan was younger and hip and clearly (to only her) way out of her league. She remembers feeling embarrassed on his behalf that he was out on a date with her. The abuse she endured in her marriage still had its tentacles inside her brain.

But after a full year and a half of dating, Nina was finally able to accept that Dan was "her person." He wasn't just some guy she was dating or even just her boyfriend. She wanted to build a future with him. So they moved in together and got engaged. They even started planning a quick and easy wedding since she didn't want to go through with a big celebration again. But then she called it off six weeks before the wedding because Nina was dealing with another bombshell she hadn't seen coming. Dan had a substantial drinking problem. And he had recently relapsed.

Nina didn't know Dan was an alcoholic until they moved in together. Discovering something so substantial about her partner after knowing him for so long wasn't only shocking, it was triggering. She started beating herself up for "picking wrong again." But this relationship was drastically different from her first marriage—even if there was still an element of unwanted surprise. Nina postponed their wedding, but she didn't give up on Dan. Instead, she supported him while he began AA and, by the fall, they were married in an intimate backyard ceremony.

Despite Dan's struggles with alcohol, Nina knew that wasn't who he really was. She shared, "I really think that my first marriage was helpful in defining that for me because Dan was a partner. He was a person I could count on, that I could rely on." As they both worked from home during the pandemic, spending countless time together, Nina felt even more secure in her choice. She finally understood all those people who referred to their spouse as their favorite person.

Over time, though, Dan started to get sick as his liver began to fail. Doctors knew he was an alcoholic who also had diabetes, but they didn't fully understand what was happening. Dan and Nina were in and out of the hospital. And one horrific morning, Nina woke up in their home to an empty bed. When she found Dan on the floor in a different part of the house, she knew he was already gone. The rest of that horrible day is hazy in her mind, but her time with Dan isn't.

When Nina took the leap to get married for a second time, she had no idea that in less than two years she would be a widow. And yet, Nina finds comfort in the fact that she has no regrets. She told me, "I wouldn't give it back. I wouldn't trade it... I wouldn't have gone back and bubbled in a different sheet on the old universal Scantron. Because I loved being with Dan. And being with Dan was phenomenal."

Considering we talked only a few months after Dan's passing, Nina doesn't know what her future will hold or if she'll ever want to get married again. But she does have clarity on what her marriage with Dan meant. Being with him helped her realize that she is fine being on her own. She doesn't *need* marriage. But a good marriage enhances the life you are already living. It's additive. She said, "I didn't need him to make me happy, but I was so much happier because he was there." And even though she is now a young widow with the rest of her life in front of her, she said, "I can take all of that with me. All of that gets to stay."

Nina's experience shows that a marriage doesn't have to last for decades for it to be transformative. It can be worth the risk even if you don't get a traditional happy ending.

After all my (failed) attempts to extinguish anxiety in my relationships, I've realized that having *some* anxiety around commitment can serve a purpose. Sara explains, "When we are entering into a committed relationship with someone, it's always a leap of faith and requires an incredible amount of trust. These are huge life decisions and I would argue they *should* make us anxious. You can take your time and ask all the right questions, but there's never a guarantee." I personally love whenever I'm given permission to feel anxious, because 1) I'm probably already feeling anxious and 2) it's a reminder that not all anxiety is bad anxiety. The good kind can actually encourage us to have tough conversations and cover all our bases. Her response also showcases the fact that no matter how much thought we put into our future with our spouses, there is always an element of hoping for the best (and preparing for the worst).

Fully understanding and embracing that we can't prevent a level of uncertainty in our lives and marriages has been extremely freeing for me. We don't have to wait around to be sure to move forward because none of us can be sure about anything. And I have put less pressure on myself to get this huge part of my life "right" because I've given up on the ability to be "right" at all. The only thing I am certain about in my marriage is that John is worth the risk of being wrong.

That said, there are always things we can do to lower the amount we are leaving to chance or change. One possible way is to try to answer the following:

QUESTIONS TO ASK YOURSELF

- Do I struggle with commitment? If yes, is there any part of my personal history that could explain why?
- What is my own personal "commitment speed" or route?
- Would I regret a 30-year marriage that ultimately ends in divorce if the majority of the time was happy and fulfilling?
- What can I do to increase my tolerance for uncertainty? How can I get more comfortable relinquishing some control over my life?
- Am I open to the idea of allowing myself and my partner to change with time and experience? Why or why not?

QUESTIONS TO DISCUSS WITH YOUR PARTNER

- What scares us the most about getting married or being married?

- Are our two commitment speeds or routes different? How so?
- Is any of our individual behavior around the relationship confusing or frustrating for the other person? Is there any additional history or context that might make it less so?
- Why am I worth the risk for you? (And vice versa.)

Now that we've learned there is no way to avoid risk in our relationships, it's time to explore another one of society's biggest questions around marriage: *When* should you do it?

5

FROM WHICH DAY FORWARD?

The "Right" Time To Get Married

One of my favorite segments in *The Bachelor/Bachelorette* franchise is called Hometown Dates. It's an episode near the end of a season where the lead goes and meets the families of the remaining (four or so) contestants. At this point, the bachelor/bachelorette has been dating their potential spouse for a little over a month and yet they are only about a week away from potentially getting engaged. For some families, this timeline makes sense given the nature of the show, and all they seem to care about is that their child doesn't get their heart broken. But for many family members, the idea that their kid might get engaged after knowing someone for such a short amount of time is completely and utterly *bonkers*. How is it possible to know someone well enough to marry them in the approximately six weeks it takes to film an entire season? You can usually bank on at least one set of parents feeling strongly enough about this to cause some serious (and juicy) on-screen drama.

This same type of skepticism can also be applied to couples on Netflix's runaway hit, *Love Is Blind*. The show tries to set couples up for a successful marriage by forcing contestants to talk for hours—through a wall—with various potential partners. Couples then pair up, meet without a wall between them, and spend multiple weeks living together. But despite the show's efforts to eliminate the "shallow" parts of partner selection, like physical attraction, it still doesn't have a great ratio of people making it to the altar (or not divorcing quickly after wrap). If you asked me, the disappointing outcome for these shows is probably because *talking* about what a life would be like together isn't the same thing as actually *sharing* one. It is one thing to thoughtfully share your trauma on TV while dressed in your best outfit on a producer-arranged date. It's another for your partner to actually witness how that trauma impacts your day-to-day life.

I bring all this up because I find it interesting that in a society that tends to be extremely cautious and judgmental about the length of time people date before getting married, so many of our most popular reality shows try to prove that *true love* doesn't require much time at all to blossom. But are these shows just tapping into a fantasy that doesn't exist in the real world? Or is time spent together not as big of a factor in building a successful marriage as most people would have you believe?

As you can see through the families of reality TV stars, there are a lot of conflicting opinions out there about how long you should date someone before it's "safe" to get married. My hot take is that the amount of time spent together is less telling than what happened during that time. Three years of a conflict-free relationship might be less revealing than a six-month relationship filled with stress and hardship because those partners have been able to see how each responds when things aren't going well. Because how someone responds to you when they aren't stressed can be drastically different than how they respond after losing their job or breaking their leg. As Jessica, the therapist from Chapter Four, points out, "healthy rupture and repair builds empathy and leads to more intimacy." We often mistake conflict as a sign of incompatibility, but conflict is inevitable. What matters more is how, or even if, you resolve that conflict. Does it bring you closer or further apart? Is your relationship evolving following conflict? Or are you just reinjuring each other? If you can't answer any of these questions because you haven't yet had a chance to really navigate conflict beyond what movie to watch, I would argue it is probably too soon to get married.

When Brianna and Isaac met junior year of high school, neither one was thinking about getting married. They just knew they enjoyed spending time together. So even when they technically broke up the summer before senior year, they kept hanging out until they were officially back together. They then decided to remain a couple despite going away to different colleges. This new period of living apart marked a shift for Brianna. Although she was around all these new people, her heart still belonged to Isaac and she took notice.

For Isaac, it was all about finding someone he could count on. By the time he moved to Brianna's hometown at 17, he had already been through a lot. As a kid he had bounced from house to house and grew up fast due to his circumstances. Brianna, and her close-knit family, added some much desired stability to his life. For the first time, he didn't fear that she would give up on him in the way so many other people had. And he was right. When Isaac got injured playing football and dropped out of college, Brianna stood by him. She wasn't attached to the idea of him one day being a professional football player. She was attached to the current version of him—even if he was in a self-described "slump."

Then Isaac found out Brianna was pregnant during her junior year of college, and knew he needed to turn his life around. He finally felt like he had something to live for outside of himself. He wanted to provide for his new family and show up as a partner. So he drove Brianna to all of her classes since her campus was hilly and she was having a hard, uncomfortable pregnancy. He got a job and even worked nights when their daughter was born so Brianna could finish her degree. If that period of time was a test of how they would work as a couple long term, they seem to have passed. Big time.

Today, Brianna recognizes that the odds were against them given their age, an unplanned pregnancy, Isaac's multiple football injuries, and Brianna's ongoing struggle with epilepsy. (She started having seizures in high school.) As teenagers, neither one had put much thought into picking each other beyond "I like you and this feels good." They weren't working off a list of what to look for in a future spouse. But by the time they got married, they had been through enough of life together to know they had something special. There was evidence that they each had the capacity and willingness to take care of each other during the lowest moments. And for them, that's all they really needed to know to make it official.

In addition to shared experiences, I also think age is another undeniable factor when it comes to how long people are together before tying the knot. Adult brains continue to significantly develop until around age 25, which arguably means it's a bit riskier to make such a major life decision in your early twenties. Not to mention that most people are still figuring out who they are in those pivotal young adult years. While it's certainly possible to grow in the same direction as your high school sweetheart-turned-young spouse, I'd imagine there is a bigger chance that your personalities and paths could still evolve or diverge later in life—which, for some people, is a risk they're willing to take. And there are plenty of happy marriages that go on to prove the risk was worth it.

As hesitant as I sometimes feel about people getting married young, despite the many success stories, I have a different mindset when it comes to older people getting hitched quickly. The older you are, the more likely you already have relationship experience and a stronger sense of self and what you want. Learning how to be in a partnership is a skill that takes time to develop. Sometimes it can take people multiple relationships to figure out how to resolve conflict or take another person's needs as seriously as their own. So if I hear about two forty-year-olds who have both had long-term relationships before getting engaged after only eight months together I tend to think: great! They finally found a connection that works for them. Because they've also had the chance to learn what doesn't, which is equally important.

According to *Brides*, the majority of modern couples date somewhere between two and five years before getting engaged. And the average age of when people get married—roughly 30.1 years old for men and 28.2 years old for women—has gone up significantly since the 1970s, when the average was 23.2 years old for men and 20.8 years old for women. While I personally think this is a shift in the right direction, there are always going to be long-term marriages that don't fit the mold and plenty of marriages that end despite following all the logical "right steps."

That's why the idea of trying to find the exact right

amount of time to date before getting married feels like a fool's errand. It completely ignores people's context and personal journeys in favor of some sort of mathematical equation that is impossible to solve. Again, I believe the *content* of your relationship—what you have gone through together—matters far more than the length. It's also important to ask ourselves if we're really out of the honeymoon phase and truly familiar with the less appealing parts of our future spouse. For example, I warned John when we started dating that I burp a lot due to my acid reflux. But he didn't understand *just how much* until we spent a lot of time together and I got more comfortable around him. (Whatever amount of burping you're imagining, it's more than that.)

We also don't want to assume that both partners have reached the same level of personal growth when they start a new relationship. When I met John, I was ready for marriage. I mean, I was literally supposed to get married to someone else that year. So the only timeline consideration for me was a period that was long enough to get to fully know each other. I didn't need more time to get to know myself or figure out what I wanted. But sometimes, people do need extra time for their own maturation—even if they've already met the person they will one day marry.

Some love stories take longer to come to fruition than others. When Rosie and Rosalina first met more than ten years ago, they were both teenagers and not yet identifying as anything other than straight. Growing up in Mexico, Rosie identified as pro-LGBTQA, but never thought she would have the opportunity to come out as gay herself. That was something only other people were allowed to do. But after years of friendship with Rosalina, her growing feelings were hard to ignore. So when Rosalina got dumped by her boyfriend, Rosie decided it was time to be vulnerable. She took a huge risk and sent an email confessing her feelings. Rosalina quickly wrote back, "We need to talk."

That talk turned into a planned weekend visit because they lived in different cities. Rosie was ecstatic. At the time, she wasn't thinking about what this monumental weekend meant in terms of her sexuality. She was thinking about what it meant for her fluttering heart. Unfortunately, her mother didn't see it that way. When she found her only daughter kissing Rosalina during the visit (their talk had clearly gone well), she declared that Rosie "had caused her a pain greater than the death of her father." Rosie's mom forced Rosalina to leave immediately and put her on a bus back home.

Despite her mom's disapproval, their budding relationship continued. Rosalina then came out as bisexual to her own mother, who stayed in bed for months recovering from the news. After seeing one parent have such a negative reaction, Rosalina kept her sexuality secret from her father for another two years. But she didn't end the relationship. They kept dating long-distance even though Rosie's mother would only let her visit Rosalina with a chaperone. A few years into their relationship, they tried to live in Rosalina's city together, but Rosie had to quit her job and move back home due to her coworkers' homophobia. So many things were stacked against them, except their desire to be together.

Then the topic of marriage started popping up and caused a rift. Rosie was a romantic who had been dreaming of her wedding since she was a little girl. She was also proudly out as a lesbian by that point despite her mother's disapproval. Rosalina, on the other hand, felt far too young to get married and was still dealing with internalized homophobia, having not fully come to grips with her own sexuality quite yet. She didn't want their relationship to be public on social media and felt incredibly anxious about PDA in conservative Mexico. Plus Rosalina was studying abroad in France at the time, so they weren't even in the same country. All these issues compounded and led Rosalina to break up with Rosie five and a half years into their relationship.

Rosalina of today refers to this decision as the biggest regret of her life. Except, in some ways, that decision led her to where she is now: happily married to Rosie. So how did they go from broken up to back together? It wasn't easy: both of them thought their relationship was truly over and behaved as such. After the breakup, Rosie was heartbroken and angry. She now had to try to date for the first time at 27 and was not having much luck. Her dream of the perfect wedding seemed further and further away.

After a full year of not speaking, Rosie and Rosalina got back in touch. It wasn't anything too meaningful, just some friendly exchanges. They also had to see each other at a concert they had bought tickets for while they were still a couple. The concert wasn't romantic because Rosalina was seeing someone else at the time. But it turned out that that other relationship helped Rosalina realize Rosie was the person she wanted to be with.

After three years of not being together, Rosalina was in a very different place than when they broke up. Back then, she'd thought marriage meant leaving her older parents all alone. It meant giving up her stable job near her childhood home. It meant making their relationship public to everyone before she felt comfortable doing so. She wasn't ready to do any of that, so she had pulled away and cut the cord. But Rosalina realized that over time, all of those things had became nonissues. She'd already left her parents on their own and accepted a job in California, and through therapy, she had come to realize that her parents weren't her responsibility. She'd also been able to process her fears around people judging their same-sex relationship. During their time apart, Rosalina had gotten to a place where she could finally give Rosie what she had always wanted, and now Rosalina wanted all those things too. Plus they were working in the same city and already seeing each other as friends—Rosalina just needed to turn it back into something more.

Waiting three years for an ex to change their perspective and circumstances so you can get back together and have a fairy-tale wedding isn't exactly an outcome you can bank on. But what made their happy ending possible is that Rosalina had the time and space to actually change and could articulate *how* she made those changes instead of just saying things would "be different" this time around to please Rosie. They hadn't been ready for the same things their first go-around, but now they were.

So ten years to the day that Rosie sent that email confessing her feelings, Rosalina planned a surprise picnic and proposed to her. Rosie then surprised Rosalina by proposing right back. She'd planned on doing something small because Rosalina doesn't like a lot of attention, while Rosalina had planned something elaborate since Rosie was a romantic. They knew how to show love to each other in the way the other person wanted.

Rosie and Rosalina's journey back to each other wasn't inevitable or without significant hurt. They also had to deal with a lot of familial and societal disapproval. Rosie's mother even tried to trick her into conversion therapy at one point. But by the time they got married, all of their parents were there in attendance (some more accepting than others). Rosie got the wedding she had always dreamed of, and Rosalina, well, Rosalina got the girl she didn't know she wanted to marry until it was almost too late.

I've come to suspect that so many of us are fixated on the timing part of the marriage conversation because it's something concrete we can measure and judge about other people. While it's often impossible to know the intricacies of a marriage you aren't a part of, it *is* possible to know how long two people dated before they got married. So if they end up getting divorced after dating for less than a year, it's tempting to say, *Well, they clearly rushed into it.* Or if a couple takes their time to get married only to break up, one can jump to, *I knew something was fishy. Why else take so long to get married?* Having what feels like tangible reasons we can point to for a marriage not working out can alleviate our own fears that if we date for a respectable amount of time, we will have a better outcome.

But as we are learning throughout this book there are far too many factors that influence a marriage's well-being for timing to take center stage. I'm not going to advise anyone to get married to someone you've known for less than six months, but I'm also not going to automatically assume those types of marriages are doomed. Personality traits, age, outside context, and pure luck likely have more influence on a marriage's well-being than choosing to commit within a certain preapproved time frame. That doesn't mean we shouldn't be thoughtful about our timing, but being thoughtful and being constrained are two different things.

So with all those hot takes in mind, here are some questions to ponder:

QUESTIONS TO ASK YOURSELF

- Do I believe there is a "right" amount of time to date before getting married? Why might I have come to this conclusion?
- Do I have a habit of judging other people for how quickly or slowly they get married? If so, is this something I want to push back against?

- What are some signs that I know someone well enough to marry them?

QUESTIONS TO DISCUSS WITH YOUR PARTNER

- How important is the timing of our marriage to you? How does it compare to other factors in our decision-making?
- Are you satisfied with how we handle conflict? If not, what are some ways we could improve?
- How will we (or did we) know we were ready for marriage?

Counting how long you've been together isn't the only role numbers play in a marriage. Which is why our next chapter is dedicated to all things finance. (See what I did there? Pretty good!)

6

TO OPEN A JOINT ACCOUNT OR NOT TO OPEN A JOINT ACCOUNT

Facing Our Finances

During the dreadful summer of 2020, my then-fiancé and I drove from Los Angeles to Colorado to enjoy some time with my parents at a rental property my dad had found online. We spent the week showing my parents my shiny new engagement ring and attempting to play pickleball without knowing any of the rules. We also spent a good amount of time discussing our upcoming wedding.

Before I met my ex-fiancé, my parents had always advised me to get a prenup. They thought it was the right decision given the nature of my work, and I agreed. My comedy partner, Gabe Dunn, and I even used to sell a mug that read "Get a Prenup" as merchandise. Prenuptial agreements were a part of my brand. So when I asked my parents during the trip how to go about getting one, I was shocked to hear they had changed their minds. Apparently, their pro-prenup agenda had been shaped by my not-so-good dating history. But now that I was marrying a trustworthy "good guy," I didn't need to worry about it. They thought I was safe with him. I did too. Until he left three months later.

Looking back, I think my parents' change of heart revealed a secret bias that lives in so many of us. We know it's smart to *always* financially protect ourselves in case things go awry. But practically, we tend to pick and choose what marriages we think need that kind of protection. Most likely due to our perceptions around the "strength" of the relationship or the "true" character of the people involved (*she's clearly a gold digger* or *he's a family man so you don't need your own source of income*). There's also a large contingent of people who view prenups as unromantic and refuse to entertain the idea at all, despite the ever-present possibility of divorce.

The controversy and prejudice around prenups points to people's resistance to look at marriage for what it truly is: a business decision. Because what's the biggest tangible difference between an unmarried couple and a married one today? Having legally linked finances.

As much as we love having money, most of us hate talking about it. But when you're planning to legally combine your life with someone, you can't avoid the green elephant in the room and what you want to do with it. In fact, openly talking about finances is one of the best ways to set your relationship (and future self) up for success. Even if doing so makes you want to vomit.

I believe one of my biggest perception shifts when it comes to modern marriage has to do with the finances of it all. Growing up, I assumed all couples shared their money and combined all their assets into a joint bank account because that's what my parents did. Shortly after I was born, my mom quit her overdemanding, underpaying job as an editor and writer on Wall Street, so I was raised in a single-income home. While my dad technically made all the money, it was never verbalized or viewed that way. My mom had access to everything and would consult with my father only about big purchases, not so he could control her, but so they could make those decisions together. When I grew up and started hearing about married couples who had separate finances and alternated who paid for dinner, I found it weird at best and unsettling at worst. Why even marry someone if you didn't merge financial resources? A lifetime of splitting the check was my nightmare, and not just because I struggle to calculate the proper tip. Keeping your accounts separate felt like an illusion of a true marriage to me and it made me wonder, "what's even the point?"

Now that I'm older, I see it all differently. The U.S. Census Bureau confirms that Americans are getting married later in life than before, which means people are entering into unions with more assets than past generations. It also means new spouses have spent a longer time living as financially independent adults before tying the knot. When my parents got married at 23 and 24, they had nothing (other than student debt). Building their wealth as a team felt natural.

By contrast, when I married John, I was 34 with multiple bank accounts, an S-Corp, a Roth IRA and investments in the stock market that I don't fully understand. Joining our finances isn't simple. So while I still enjoy and embrace having the mentality of "what's mine is yours," I've decided I don't need that to be reflected on paper. It is too much of a headache to officially merge everything, especially since we've already been living together and making it work despite separate accounts. This technically-separate-but-mentally-shared approach has continued to work well for us for now, but I remain open to change in the future. Especially if one of us has to take time off for childcare at some point.

With this possibility in mind, I decided to seek some insight from Stacy Francis, president and CEO of the financial advisory firm Francis Financial, about the idea of separate or joint accounting for married couples. One interesting idea she offered was that if you do join accounts, you can, and probably should, still consider the assets you enter into a marriage with as "premarital" money and treat it like a lockbox. With this system, she says, "You can change that money around, you can do anything you want with the way it's invested, but don't add more money to it," since that would make it harder to claim as yours if you end up getting divorced.

Announcing to your new spouse, "I love you and I'm also going to keep all my premarital money in my own bank account" is a hard thing to do. But so is taking a risk on joining your life with another person. It's okay to have some safety measures in place before you dive off the metaphorical cliff into matrimony. Especially considering we all have different histories and trigger points and some people might require more measures to feel comfortable. Different states also have different levels of protection for married couples who divorce, which can impact what extra steps you feel you do or don't need to take. What's most important, regardless of where you live or your level of concern, is to try to find partners who are comfortable with whatever it is we *do* need. Even if those needs inevitably change with time and circumstance.

Personally, another part of my reluctance to make any big changes to our financial status quo is that thinking about all this stuff makes me feel not only anxious, but also dumb. I'm not financially savvy and I'm also hyperaware that money conversations can be deeply emotional in ways we aren't always equipped to handle. As Stacy points out, "Many of us were never raised to feel comfortable talking about money" and, as a result, the topic is avoided—only for so many couples to later split up due to financial issues. Kathleen Burns Kingsbury, a wealth psychology expert, refers to this avoidance as *money silence*. And it's getting in the way of having healthy relationships. (Clearly, I am not alone in my reluctance to dive into spreadsheets and uncomfortable conversations.)

But *why* is it so darn difficult to discuss this part of our lives with the person we trust with our time, heart, and body? Kathleen explains that in addition to us thinking it is "rude" to directly talk about finances, there is this belief that many people have that "if I talk about money, I'll look stupid because everybody else has it figured out." (Guilty!) To complicate matters even further, Marguerita Cheng, a certified financial planner, notes that money symbolizes different things to different people. For some, it equates to "peace of mind," while for others it is a means of control and power, or freedom and flexibility. So when you try to initiate a conversation about money with your partner, you can't even go into it assuming you're talking about the same stakes or implications. Money is a loaded topic, regardless of your background.

I asked some of the experts about ways to make these conversations easier. Dominique Broadway, a personal finance expert and money therapist, says she often advises clients to have "money dates," when they dress up, go to a nice restaurant and talk about their finances and financial goals. If that feels like too much, or the idea of dressing up to talk about current interest rates seems like a drag, shorter planned conversations can work just as well. Dominique and her husband chat for at least 20 minutes each Sunday to make sure they're on the same financial page. No matter what setting you decide, having a time set aside on a regular basis can help the subject become more comfortable. It also means you aren't talking about money only in times of stress, so your association with these conversations will probably become less charged over time.

While it's good to know these talks can get easier with practice, figuring out how to initiate conversations about finances with a new partner can still be daunting. Stacy refers to it as getting "financially naked," which might be less fun than getting physically naked, but is equally important. Before you marry someone, you want to know not only their spending habits, but also their financial goals, debts, assets, and expectations. Kathleen says it can be productive if partners start the conversation by sharing a "financial success." This sets the tone better than opening with your student debt, or your habit of paying way too much to get your nails done because you lack the fine motor skills to do them yourself. (Just me?)

According to Kathleen, it can be worthwhile to ease into these tough conversations by not immediately diving into the nitty-gritty of the numbers in your bank accounts. Instead of grilling your partner about their last credit card statement, broader, more personal questions can peel back where your partner's perspective is coming from. For example, "How did your parents talk about money? How do you feel about money? What are some things you wish you had done differently financially?" What are their financial goals? Maybe they want to buy a house one day, retire early or, like my husband, they have an inexplicable yearning to purchase a $14,000 iPitch machine even though they don't play professional baseball. The *New York Times*'s viral "13 Questions to Ask Before Getting Married" includes some helpful, playful questions like, "What's the most you would be willing to spend on a car, a couch, and shoes?" These types of discussions can reveal your partner's priorities very quickly. Obviously, no one can know for sure what their financial future will look like, but having a clear understanding of what they *want* it to look like makes it easier to know your pain points and alignments.

I've also found that having these kinds of difficult conversations can reveal aspects of your partner's psyche that are useful to know. When I first started dating my ex-fiancé, I initiated a frank conversation about money in an effort to be mature and proactive about our potential future together. I didn't want the topic to become taboo, so I smashed through pleasantries with a metaphorical bat and a list of my own financial goals. We started talking about what it would look like to have children, and I said I wouldn't feel comfortable having kids unless we hit a certain amount of joint income. You may be thinking, that's all valid and good, except the amount I said was, well, completely ridiculous. It was far too high, and it immediately hit a nerve with him because it seemed to insinuate that I was expecting a lifestyle he might not be able to provide. In reality, I just had a skewed sense of what it actually costs to raise children due to my privileged background and my tendency to worry. (I was particularly panicked about finding myself in a position where I had a child I couldn't comfortably afford.) So all that background mixed with the financial instability of my chosen career and the expense of living in Los Angeles caused me to spit out a desired joint income of $400,000.

I know.

I know.

I know.

That number is ludicrous and pretty unattainable for most people. And over the course of our relationship I quickly realized that and took it back. The problem was, I don't think he believed me.

It's normal to have bumps in the road when discussing this stuff. Given the touchy nature of the subject, people can—correctly or incorrectly—infer a lot of judgment or disappointment from their partner about their income or potential earnings. I don't think we can successfully prevent that kind of misstep from ever taking place. But what we can do is commit to working through it when it happens. I realized my mistake and I did my best to repair the damage.

This experience also made me realize how important it is to have a partner who allows room for growth. I don't want to be held to something I said one time for the rest of my life, especially if I've loudly announced I've since changed my mind. The whole point of having these kinds of talks is to get a dialogue going and come to an eventual place of agreement and/or understanding. It's essential to create an environment with each other where it feels like it is safe to share, even if what we share is initially shocking or needs to be reconsidered.

But creating that kind of environment is tricky, especially when you've had past experiences that didn't go well. Maybe one partner has their hackles up and always expects the worst outcome. I certainly felt that way when I found myself in a near identical conversation with John a few years after I spouted that ridiculous number to my ex (which may or may not have led to the slow demise of my first engagement. Not that I'll ever know!). We had come to the conversation from another angle this time— my shortly lived fear that John didn't want to marry me— but the general sentiment was the same. John expressed for the first time that he needed clarity on my feelings about having kids before we got engaged so he could better envision our life together. His curiosity made sense, because while I had said I was open to kids, I also made a lot of jokes about *not* wanting to have them. (Love to repeatedly share my deep-rooted fears about parenthood and pregnancy through the thin veneer of humor! It's a foolproof plan that no one can see through immediately.)

In that moment, I was terrified to share that my decision around whether I want to have kids is directly tied to our financial security. And given that our careers as writers are more of the freelance variety than the stable variety, I wasn't sure if we would ever get to a place where I'd feel comfortable bringing new life into the world. The decision to have children given the current economy, wage inequality, job instability, and the increasing threat of climate change, isn't the same decision our parents or grandparents had to make when they got married and started family planning. With the collapse of the middle class, what were once expected milestones (buying a home, having two children, being able to retire at 65) have become less attainable. We are all in uncharted waters, and I feel the pressure of that reality all the time.

The good news is that this conversation went better the second time around. Instead of focusing on a number, I tried to focus on my feelings and anxiety about the possibility of having a child we might not be able to afford. I talked through different options of what I would be comfortable with, including my desire to be able to take maternity leave even though I work for myself and wouldn't have any income during that time. It wasn't a fun conversation, and I was terrified the entire time that because my stance was not "I want to have children *no matter what*," the man I loved would reject me. But that didn't happen.

What did happen was the beginning of an ongoing conversation about when and if we are going to have kids. Most big life decisions aren't decided in one moment. Instead, they are a series of conversations and check-ins and even healthy debates, because sometimes we can sway each other's opinions through new information or a different perspective. Our discussion laid the groundwork and helped us better understand each other's starting positions. And the work isn't over. Since we don't have a magic number in mind to signal when it's suddenly financially sound for me to get pregnant, we will have to continue to talk about our current earnings, our potential earnings, and our priorities. Maybe one day we'll move out of Los Angeles to prioritize having a family. Maybe we won't. But it is only through getting financially naked with each other time and time again that we'll be able to determine what is the right decision for us.

So many people will tell you that you have to be on the exact same page about having children before getting married, but what if you are both ambivalent? What if you both only want to procreate under certain circumstances but not others? We have to allow space for and normalize collaborative decision-making *within* a marriage and not just before when it comes to family planning.

It's also been useful for us to see our friends start to have children and realize it's possible to successfully raise a family in different circumstances than how we both grew up. I'm realizing that getting financially naked with your social circle to see what's going on in other homes can be a great resource because you can learn from each other's experiences. Even if you need some social lubrication to get these conversations started.

As uncomfortable as some conversations may be, there are definitely financial benefits to tackling life as a duo. One of which is taking advantage of something called the economies of scale. In the context of a romantic relationship, the economies of scale is basically the idea that things become less expensive because you are splitting it with another person. Like the power bill when you live alone versus the power bill when you cohabit. Suddenly, the amount you individually pay each month is half the price! In many ways, when you partner up, you get to live the life of two for the price of one (or maybe one and a half). There are clear benefits, including being able to pool resources to collectively increase your quality of life (and savings account).

But what about single-income households? Even if this is often the right choice for couples, especially when they have children, can both people feel financially safe when only one of them gets a paycheck? In a world that values money above, well, life, is it possible for there *not* to be an uneven power dynamic in this type of marriage? And if it is unavoidable, how are we supposed to navigate the imbalances when only one partner has an outside income?

One approach, according to Marguerita, is for the stay-at-home partner—who is often also a stay-at-home parent—to have extra protections in place in case the marriage doesn't work out. For example, a couple can make sure the stay-at-home partner has their own retirement account because, while they might not be getting paid for their time, they are working. When meeting with her clients, she often makes a point to stop and explain the financial benefits of having a stay-at-home partner because "the only economic benefit isn't just bringing in a paycheck." In many cases, it means the couple probably doesn't have to pay someone else to manage the household or care for their children. That is a tangible, financial contribution

that should always be openly acknowledged and appreci-
ated to prevent an unfair power structure from forming.
It's also nice to say "thank you" to each other a bunch!
Who doesn't love a thank you? I could bathe in them.

Sometimes, though, words aren't enough. And what you
really need to feel secure is a binding contract in the form
of a prenup or postnup (which is basically the same thing,
but determined after the marriage instead of before). Stacy
believes that out of all marriage dynamics, it's most important to have a prenup when only one person works to
protect the stay-at-home partner. And if that arrangement
is established *after* the marriage, then you should immediately get a postnup. While the majority of this book is
gender neutral, I do think it's important to note here that
women have historically stayed at home more often and
have found themselves financially screwed if the marriage
ends. Having seen this time and time again, Stacy says,
"I'm a big proponent of women trying to keep their career.
And even if you don't keep your career during the years
when you're raising children, having your toe in the job
market, working on your skills, staying in your network
is really important. You want to make sure that if you do
return to the workforce, that you don't find yourself completely at a loss with no career options." If staying in the
workforce isn't a viable option, for whatever reason, having a prenup or postnup can still be a protective measure,
even if you don't plan on needing it.

Despite all the stigma and superstition surrounding prenups, I've learned that getting one is a lot like getting car

insurance. You don't get car insurance because you *plan* to get into an accident. You get it so that if you get into an accident, it doesn't destroy your life. Prenups and post-nups serve the same function. They give you a road map for what will happen if the marriage ends. They make the harrowing process of getting divorced a bit easier, because so much has already been worked out during a time of peace and mutual respect. And, as Marguerita points out, they can also help you determine how you plan to handle additional items like a long-term care event or inheritances during the course of your marriage. They do not have to be limited to the potential division of financial assets.

The process of negotiating a prenup with your soon-to-be spouse can also be a valuable learning experience. Stacy explains, "How you're treated in that prenup is also how you're treated in your marriage. So if you're being given a draconian prenup that does not treat you well, I think that that's something that you really have to con-sider, of whether or not this is someone who you truly feel has your best interests at heart." To me, a draconian prenup would divide assets extremely unfairly and make it so one partner would have a significantly negative life-style change in the wake of a split. One way to advocate for yourself during the prenup/postnup process is to make sure you have your own lawyer review the document on your behalf. You also never want to sign under pressure. As Stacy said, this contract isn't just establishing logistics. It's also establishing how you feel in your relationship.

I was cognizant of all this as John and I began the process of looking into getting a prenup. We didn't want anything fancy, but I still wanted clear protections if either one of us ever took off work for childcare. After we each spent an hour on the phone with different attorneys, we came back together and talked through our options. It turns out that California has really great laws in place to protect nonworking spouses and fairly split assets acquired during the marriage. Simply put, due to its community property laws, getting a divorce in California would be a more equitable experience than in other states. After we learned this, as well as the cost of getting a prenup (somewhere in the $3000–6000 range, if everything went super smoothly), we decided that we didn't need to get a prenup. But if we ever decide to leave California, we will get a postnup to make sure we have the same protections regardless of where we live.

After my experience with my ex-fiancé, I had felt certain that I needed to get a prenup *no matter what*. But by allowing myself to lead with facts and not emotion, I was able to realize this was the best financial decision for us as a couple. The worry in this approach, which my retired lawyer of a father was quick to point out, is that sometimes people change. And what happens if in five years we want to leave the state only for one of us to suddenly refuse to get the postnup? If this betrayal were to happen, I think, like Stacy mentioned, it would speak to a bigger issue at play in our relationship than the logistics of a cross-state move. Regardless, joining your assets is always a risk, which is why the bigger picture of financial decisions often boils down to the importance of trust and flexibility in your marriage.

Back when Barbara got married, prenups weren't a thing. At least not for regular people who didn't have billions of dollars to protect. At 26 years old, she went into her marriage thinking it would last forever and all their money would be shared. Part of that ended up being true. During the 20 years Barbara was married to Gary, she never once felt like the money he earned with his high-paying job was his. It was theirs. And after Barbara quit her accounting job while pregnant, she took over the family's finances and paid all the bills. But after 17 good years with Gary, things started to fall apart. And by the time they officially divorced when she was 47, Barbara knew Gary was not the person she wanted to spend the rest of her life with.

While the decision to separate was amicable, it wasn't something that could be accomplished overnight. Their only daughter, Lucy, was a junior in high school and Barbara didn't want to disrupt such a vital time with this news. So she put off telling Lucy for about five months and based her settlement around what she thought would be best for her. Part of that was not spending a ton of money on lawyers in a lengthy divorce. Instead, Barbara and Gary worked with a mediator. They even came in with an agreement already worked out (although the mediator had to point out some areas they had overlooked, which is natural due to this being their first divorce and all).

Since Lucy was still under 18, Gary had to legally provide child support, but they also decided he would provide alimony until Barbara sold their house. She wanted to stay in it through Lucy's high school graduation and first year of college, in part because her own parents had sold her childhood home right after she left for school and it was a tough experience she didn't want replicated for her own daughter. (She also astutely remarked that whether a child is 12 or 32, their parents' divorce will still affect them in a sizable way.) However, it was what Gary and Barbara decided to do *after* those first few years that was particularly interesting.

Instead of continuing to share Gary's earnings through alimony, Gary proposed the idea of giving Barbara a lump sum after she sold the house. At first, Barbara was put off by this suggestion. Was he trying to give her a bad deal? But once Gary explained his reasoning, she understood. He told her, "Look, I know you. You're not going to want to feel a dependence on me for the rest of your life... And quite frankly, I don't want to be responsible to you for the rest of my life." So after two decades of financially sharing everything, they both decided it would be in their best emotional interest to completely cut the cord.

From that moment on, Barbara had a lump sum of money that she had to make last the rest of her life because she didn't want to return to the workforce. She had been out of the game too long and knew her potential earnings wouldn't be worth it. Luckily, that sum was high enough that she wasn't worried about being financially insecure.

But it did mean some lifestyle changes. Most notably, she had to start paying for her own insurance, and as the cost had gone up her level of plan has gone down. (At the time of our interview, Medicare hadn't yet activated for her, but was due to soon.) She'd also invested her money over the years, both on her own and with the help of professionals. But not having an additional income has made her more cautious in her investments because she couldn't afford to take big risks and lose it all. Even if those riskier investments occasionally bring bigger gains.

As Barbara set up a new life for herself, a realization dawned on her. She didn't want to get married again. She had grown to love having her own space and keeping odd hours. Breakfast was no longer a social occasion but a time when she could eat whatever she wanted by herself. But this epiphany didn't mean she wanted to stay single. Which brings us to Mark, her boyfriend of seven years. Who she refuses to marry or even live with.

Barbara's trajectory from a woman who felt old for getting married at 26 to a wife who found it weird when other couples didn't share finances to a divorcée with no interest in legally binding herself to another person (again) is an important one. Barbara grew up in a time when there weren't that many options for couples. That time is no longer. While Mark would prefer to get married or at least live together, Barbara knows that's not the right decision for her, and he respects her enough not to push. Or, perhaps, not push too much. When Mark occasionally brings up all the money they would save by not having separate residences, Barbara replies, "there's more to life than money."

One of the big differences between seriously dating someone and marrying them is that money doesn't take up the same amount of space in your relationship. During Barbara's marriage she was keenly aware of Gary's income and set the budget for the household with any huge expense being a point of discussion and deliberation. Now, Barbara doesn't even know how much money Mark has or makes. It doesn't directly affect her. She doesn't need to ask those tough questions. Instead, she lets him pay for most things when they're together because he wants to, and she tries to occasionally contribute without making it a big deal. When it comes to splitting costs, they have fallen into an old-school gendered dynamic that works for them. But when it comes to everything else, they are creating their own rules—and breakfasts.

Just because Barbara doesn't want to get married again, doesn't mean she is anti-marriage. Lucy is newly married to a great guy and Barbara is thrilled for them to build a life together. But she doesn't want Lucy to stop working like she did. She knows her daughter and she knows Lucy's work is important to her. She thinks Lucy will be able to have kids and keep her career, which Barbara recognizes isn't an option for everyone. If it is possible, though, Barbara thinks it's smart to keep working because it provides financial security. She knows people who "stay in lousy relationships because they feel like they're stuck financially." And she doesn't want that for her daughter. Or herself.

If you haven't figured it out yet, I am not good with money. I mean, I love having it. And I love spending it (mostly on soft clothes and frozen yogurt). But I don't like thinking about how to use it strategically and I'm still not sure how to properly utilize and claim my business expenses despite my accountant and my father begging me to keep track of such things. (Sorry, Brian! And Dad!)

John, on the other hand, has a knack for money and investments. He once pretended to be too sick to go to high school so he could stay home and buy Apple stock at exactly the right time. His birthday present when he was 16 included getting his own bank account so he could begin a life of financial freedom. Meanwhile, when my bank started to fail in April 2023, I just sort of "waited it out" until it (luckily) got bought by JP Morgan.

But as much as I would like to hand all financial decisions over to John, I know that I need to remain (or actually *become*) an active participant in our financial health and decision-making. Stacy points out that in heterosexual relationships women tend to outlive their male spouses, so even if your marriage makes it to the finish line, you might still find yourself solely responsible for your finances one day. That's why it's important not to stay in the dark or assume that since your partner has a better understanding of it, they should take care of it all. Not knowing anything about our finances would put me in a dangerous spot if something were to happen to John. As Kathleen explains, "If you're not financially dominant, if you're not the one that's interested or as knowledgeable, you still need to be involved periodically because you need to know where the accounts are."

Luckily, financial literacy is something that can be learned. There are a lot of free resources out there to help us learn how to manage money if it's not something that comes naturally (or with any interest). Stacy herself founded a charity called Savvy Ladies that helps women get more, you guessed it, savvy with their finances. She believes that "one of the biggest financial vulnerabilities women have is getting married," because, in heterosexual marriages, often "the husband is taking care of the money and the wife is in charge of running the household, which leaves her financially vulnerable." This same dynamic can also potentially occur in queer relationships with a single income. Luckily, we can combat this potential inequality by making sure both partners, in all marriages, are active and equally involved in financial decisions, from agreeing on big purchases to deciding how much to spend versus save. Even if you are still keeping separate accounts.

One of the reasons it can feel overwhelming to learn about and participate in finances is that there is no absolute "right" way to go about navigating it all. When I asked the experts questions like, "should you merge investment accounts" or "should you pay for each other's debts once you're married" they were hesitant to give definitive answers. Dominique admits, "There is no one size fits all… That's why I think it's important for you to sit down with your partner and see: How do they want to do this thing?

And don't feel pressured that this is the only way that it can be done. I think that's the most important thing for people to realize. We're in a whole new world now." And since that new world is filled with student debt, couples need to proactively figure out what works for them.

As with the other marital topics throughout this book, personal finances are adapting to modern times. This means there is much more flexibility around relationship arrangements. A single-income home with shared finances and no protections for the stay-at-home spouse is no longer the only or default option. You and your spouse get to decide what works best for your values, lifestyle, and relationship in an increasingly insecure world instead of simply falling into an outdated status quo.

Being on the same page about money is one of the (many) things that is easier said than done. Especially if you enter into the partnership with totally different spending habits. What exactly do you do if one person is a saver and the other is a spender? Are you doomed to argue about money until the end of time—or the dissolution of your marriage?

Kathleen doesn't think so. She believes that instead of viewing that difference as a source of conflict, we should try to look for the strengths in our partner's perspective. Savers, for example, are likely good at allotting for an emergency fund, budgeting, and weighing the risk and value of significant costs. That's a valuable skill to have, but it's also less fun because, um, most fun things cost money. Spenders can help their partners to be more spontaneous, enjoy more experiences, and not be so rigid around spending. Meanwhile, savers can help spenders better prepare for big purchases and avoid the pitfalls of not having an adequate savings account for emergencies.

While these different approaches might seem like big lifestyle variances, it's important to realize that they don't prevent couples from being able to agree on what fundamental values matter most. For example, perhaps both partners prioritize their children's happiness, even if they go about it in different ways. For the saver, this value might result in them putting money away each month for a college fund. For the spender, the same value might lead them to spending money on a sleepaway camp. By understanding that you have the same end goal, it's easier to not resent or judge each other because you have a shared objective to work from. A compromise in this situation might look like putting a bit less in the college savings account each month to pay for a half-session of a reasonably priced sleepaway camp, attending to both the present and future needs of the child. As Marguerita points out, "If everyone saved all the time, they may not enjoy life. If everyone spent all the time, they still wouldn't enjoy life." It's important to find the healthy medium of living in the moment and enjoying your finances, but also knowing you can take care of yourself and your future in the "longer-term"—which will be defined differently from couple to couple.

Sometimes, the right balance requires a bit more work,

negotiation, and frequent conversations about money between partners. It can help to set up certain systems like having the spender put their portion of the rent into a designated account right after being paid. That way neither party has to worry it will get spent somewhere else. Dominique said it best: "A lot of people who are bad with money, they know...but awareness is the first step." As long as the spending partner isn't defensive about this quality, the saver can help establish certain limitations "so they don't self-destruct."

Marguerita offered another possible solution—to set aside certain amounts for purchases that have historically caused conflict. She explains that when working with clients, "if the husband thinks she spends too much on entertainment and the wife thinks he spends too much on tech gadgets, we find out what is an appropriate number. We set that aside... That's money that they can spend on their hobbies and respective pursuits without blowing up the finances." Basically, what she's describing here is having a yearly budget that includes *fun*, which is personally the only budget I can get behind without wanting to scream endlessly into the void.

One financial question that is probably on all our minds given the recent recessions and unprecedented inflation is, how much should we be planning for a financial disaster? If we don't know what's going to happen in the future, should we always be prepared for the worst (i.e., unemployment, medical debt and/or an alien invasion that weakens our local currency)? When I asked Kathleen this very question, she shared, "I don't think of financial planning as planning for disaster... I think of it more as like, taking care of my partner." I love this reframe. Suddenly your savings account isn't simply doomsday prep, it's a love letter to each other (albeit one made of numbers and not words).

I think this mindset of caring for each other can extend into all aspects of our finances. Getting a prenup or keeping your accounts separate no longer feels like an attack against the strength of your marriage when you view it as a way to show your affection by making the other person feel safe and secure. It also speaks to your commitment and respect for each other not just as spouses but as individual people in a world where bad stuff happens. Sure, it's romantic to surprise your spouse with flowers. But nothing says "I care" more than a partner making sure you'll continue to get their pension benefits after they die by filling out the right form. Or by allowing you to keep a separate account for all the money you individually entered the marriage with so you don't ever feel trapped. It's hard to feel completely safe with someone if they aren't looking out for you in all areas of your life.

Sometimes it can take time to get to a place where merging your finances is the right and respectful decision for both spouses. For Claire and Rachel, it took approximately ten years. Instead of having joint accounts, for the past decade they were using a system where Claire would write Rachel checks or give her cash to pay for expenses or anything she owed her. This haphazard arrangement makes sense once you know their context. While Claire had a great, high-paying job as a lawyer, when she first met Rachel, Claire also had a horrible credit score that she was terrified to tell her new girlfriend about.

For a significant portion of her adult life, Claire had undiagnosed ADD. And the intersection of mental disorders and poor financial decisions is not only significant but often underdiscussed. Claire explains, "One of the biggest things for women who have ADD is impulsivity, and that can really show up in finances. And so I had years of bad finance management and a really bad credit score."

By the time she met Rachel she was diagnosed and in treatment, but her credit score hadn't yet recovered. She was worried how this information might go over since it would impact their ability to do things like rent an apartment together. But once Claire initiated the conversation—and it went well—it suddenly became easier to talk about finances in general. This experience shows that understanding someone's financial history might include learning more about their mental health history. Certain disorders (including ADHD and any disorder that includes mania or hypomania) are often linked to impulsive spending. Similarly, money struggles can aggravate anxiety and depression. That's why frank conversations about money can, and often should, lead to frank discussions about both partners' mental health.

Part of the reason Rachel wasn't overly thrown by Claire's financial history is how clearly motivated Claire was to change and improve her credit score. Rachel also understood the circumstances that had led to the situation and appreciated that Claire had been upfront and honest about it. It was also fortuitous that while Claire struggled with this part of her life, Rachel was well-versed in finances. This skillset made Rachel feel better about her overall role in the relationship even though her salary isn't as high as Claire's. Rachel is a perfect example of how the financial contributions partners make to a marriage aren't just cold hard cash (or direct deposits). Over the years, Rachel has been more in charge of paying bills and has taken on the bulk of the domestic work. This arrangement allows Claire to work long hours and, to be blunt, make a lot of money. They each bring different strengths to the table.

While they allow logic to dictate many of their financial decisions, Claire admitted to letting her emotions guide one major one: she refused to get a prenup. Legally, she understands the value, but personally, she said, "It just seemed to me that as soon as you entertain thoughts about a prenup, you've entertained thoughts about what if it doesn't work out. It's a potential out. And I didn't want us to have a potential out." This is an unusual take for a lawyer to have, but it reveals how common it is for our instincts and thoughts about marriage to not necessarily align with our instincts and thoughts about everything else. So even though Rachel had been initially curious about getting one, mainly in order to protect certain inheritances from her parents, she ultimately agreed to get married without one because of what it symbolized for Claire.

This decision was probably made easier because Claire has gone out of her way to make it clear that she will never lay claim to Rachel's inheritance. To Claire, whatever Rachel inherits will be Rachel's alone, even if that's not how they view every other part of their finances. Even though Claire has no intention of getting divorced, she explicitly told their new investment adviser to not count Rachel's future inheritance as part of their shared assets. That is her way of protecting and loving Rachel. It might seem strange that we can view marriage as forever, share our homes and our lives with our partners and still see certain financial assets as separate. But strange doesn't mean wrong. Rachel and Claire have always followed what feels right for them, even as it changes with time and rising credit scores.

I went into this chapter assuming that in addition to the risks, there were major financial benefits to being married. Who hasn't heard all the pontifications about the appeal of filing your taxes as a couple? *The tax breaks! Oh the glorious tax breaks!* But then none of my experts even brought this up. And when I asked about it, it seems not to be a cut-and-dried benefit for every couple, but more of an annoying case-by-case situation. (For example, if there is a huge salary difference between partners, they might file separately so the lower-earner can get more deductions.) The risks, though, seemed universal—like how all couples become responsible for each other's credit card debt if both names are on the account. And in general, marriage always puts you at risk of becoming a victim of financial infidelity (when your spouse intentionally lies to you about money in some way). Other than being able to share health insurance—which should be a universal right and not tied to employment, but don't get me started on that—the *potential* disadvantages seem to shine quite as brightly.

But just because the potential disadvantages are terrifying if you don't properly protect yourself, we can't overlook the most impactful benefit: the power of teamwork. Which, despite sounding like it belongs on a bumper sticker, is actually quite beautiful when you step back and think about it. Dominique explains that for many couples getting married can feel like, "Now I have a true partner, a true teammate in this and we are all in and I'm putting my money in and they're putting their money in and now it's two of us against the world." It can feel empowering to not be the only one working toward a financial goal. She also pointed out that this approach helps people reach some of their goals faster because larger merged accounts mean you can invest more aggressively. Or you can get a higher line of credit because you have more shared assets to leverage. In addition to these tangible benefits, I also think there can be immense emotional relief in simply not having to handle it alone.

Naturally, this relief is likely even stronger in today's economy, where millennials and Gen Z no longer have the same level of career stability as past generations might have had. Gone is the age of working for the same company for decades while being able to buy a two-story home for $7 (or whatever houses cost in the '80s). People are having to job hop much more frequently, and many salaries aren't being appropriately increased with the higher cost of living. With this heightened financial insecurity, it's extra helpful to have another person in the trenches with you.

It's also important to remember that while many relationships do often have one person as the primary or sole provider, the current economic environment often leads to "seesaw marriages," where the higher earner fluctuates back and forth between the partners over the years. Under this dynamic, perhaps the higher-salaried partner is taking planned time off to go to graduate school, or one of the partners is dealing with unplanned unemployment. Sometimes it's a conscious decision to prioritize one person's career for a period and other times it's simply circumstantial. Either way, being part of a pair allows for far more flexibility than if you are solely responsible for your financial health.

But in order for a seesaw marriage to work, Kathleen notes, you have to have team spirit. There can't be any ego around who is making more. Any win should be seen as a win for both of you. Unfortunately, this type of mindset can be harder to achieve if you tie your self-worth to your income. Which is hard not to do in the capitalist hellscape we call society. Learning not to "measure your self-worth by your net worth," as Marguerita puts it, is a valuable tool that won't just dramatically improve your internal world—

it will allow you to feel like equal partners in your marriage regardless of which way the seesaw swings.

With this new mindset in mind (if not fully activated yet), here are some questions worth pondering:

QUESTIONS TO ASK YOURSELF:

- What does money symbolize to me? How has my upbringing or environment shaped those beliefs?
- Which "money talks" am I uncomfortable talking about directly, and why those specific areas? Is this something I want to push through and change?
- Am I a spender or a saver? Or do I fall somewhere in the middle?
- How strong is my financial literacy? If this is an area of weakness, should I be learning more?
- How has my mental health interacted or interfered with my finances over the course of my life?

QUESTIONS TO DISCUSS WITH YOUR PARTNER:

- What differences do we have when it comes to how we view and use money?
- Are there any big purchases or life goals that we want to collectively start saving for?
- Is there anything about my financial history or spending habits that makes you nervous or uncomfortable?

- Do we want to get a prenup or postnup? Why or why not?
- Are we adequately acknowledging nonsalary-based contributions either one of us is making toward the relationship?
- Do we want to use a financial planner to help us achieve our financial goals?
- How can we best care for each other financially?

The (green) elephant in the room is officially out of the way. Now we can explore a way less charged topic that everyone is super chill about discussing: couples therapy. See you there!

7

SHARING YOUR LIFE (WITH A MENTAL HEALTH PROFESSIONAL)

Utilizing Couples Therapy

I have been in and out of therapy since I was four years old. I had a crush on one of my old therapist's sons in high school and as I sat next to him in geometry class, I would secretly think to myself, *I've been in your house!* (His father had a home office.) When my mental health began to deteriorate freshman year of college, my parents said I was allowed to stay in California only if I started seeing a therapist again. When I got engaged (the first time), one of the people I wanted to tell the most was my then therapist of nearly a decade. (I sent a text, but she was so excited she called me!) I have sung the praises of therapy publicly, privately, and likely in my sleep. But, when my ex-fiancé brought up the idea of us going to couples therapy during a pivotal relationship discussion one month before he walked out, I scoffed.

Yep. I scoffed. Maybe not audibly, but certainly internally. At that stage, I had convinced myself that the growing distance between us was due to what I perceived to be mental health struggles and the horror of being alive during a pandemic. In my measly defense, he had also assured me *I* wasn't the problem. And my newly learned secure attachment style believed him. So couples therapy didn't seem like the right solution to fix whatever was going on with him because it seemed like a problem with *him* not *us*.

And that, my friends, is what we call a big mistake.

I've tried really hard to not beat myself up over his abandonment because it's pretty impossible to prevent something you don't see coming. It was my ex's responsibility to share the existence and depth of his doubts with me. But, it was also my job as his partner to pay attention and notice his bid for help—even if it was brief and easy to miss. Years later, I still find myself questioning the choice to deflect his suggestion, and I think my resistance came from a place of stigmatization and misinformation. (Public enemies number 1 and 2!) As much as I was a proponent of individual therapy, I still thought of couples therapy as a symbol of failure. It was a place for dysfunctional, miserable couples to yell at each other. If we went to couples therapy, it would signify something big and scary that I didn't want to face. Couples therapy was for other people, not *me* (a person who has had many mental health crises and requires medication to make life more tolerable). Look, stigma runs deep. Even in mental health advocates.

Luckily, my views on this topic have since completely changed. As I learned more about the process and intention of couples therapy, I've come to realize it's a resource that *all* couples can benefit from. (Or at least all couples who are in the position to afford it, since it's often prohibitively expensive. But that is a rant for later.)

One of our many problems in society is that we talk a lot about how to treat problems once they exist, but not enough about the power of prevention. Thankfully, younger generations seem to be more willing to use and normalize therapy as a resource than previous generations. And not to come on too strong with the hard sell, but going to premarital counseling is one of the best ways to set your marriage up for success and avoid potential problems, even if it's only for a short time. One way to think about premarital counseling is that it's like changing your bathing suit right after getting out of the pool: you aren't giving yourself enough time for a yeast infection to fester because you are taking preventive action against it. Or, you know, a different metaphor that is less gross. Like brushing your teeth to avoid cavities! Either way, I think you see my point: it would benefit all of us to shift away from the mindset that couples therapy is a terrible outcome that should be avoided until absolutely necessary, and instead start to view it as a helpful part of the marriage process.

So in an effort to not just talk the talk, John and I did ten premarital sessions with a very nice therapist over Zoom leading up to our wedding. Out of respect for John's privacy, I'm not going to share the details of what we've discussed, but what I will say is that despite being an individual therapy veteran, couples therapy does feel remarkably different. I had more unease going in and was worried that there would be unexpected bombshells about how terrible I am as a person and partner (*Hello, Anxiety! So nice for you to always be here!*). Luckily, that didn't happen. Instead, I found myself gaining far more from the experience than I had anticipated.

As you can probably guess, John and I had already covered all the big, important topics on our own because I, you know, write books about this stuff and love to talk. But there is something powerful and unique about sharing your story in front of a neutral third party. It ended up revealing more layers than we had been able to get to on our own. Or maybe it just allowed me to hear what he'd already told me in a clearer way. Couples therapy also provided a safe space to continue some ongoing conversations we'd been having about our future while getting additional insight from a professional. And perhaps most importantly, it forced us to set aside one hour a week to focus on us and what we want to build together. Even when a session was tough, we always left feeling closer to each other. Probably because we both cared enough about our relationship to have a tough session on a Sunday morning when we could have been at brunch.

One of my biggest *aha* moments about relationships was realizing that it's entirely unrealistic to expect two people with different backgrounds, families, and communication styles to *instinctively* know how to be in a healthy relationship together. We tend to assume that couples who need outside help are doing something "wrong," but viewing it this way is like expecting someone to know how to put together a complex desk without any instructions. Sometimes, you might be able to figure it out on your own, but more often than not you're going to need to watch a YouTube tutorial. Or, like me, ask your partner to watch a YouTube tutorial and then explain it back to you.

Despite my personal breakthrough, most people continue to expect the "right" relationship to be easy. Consequently, the idea of using couples therapy as a tool to strengthen your bond instead of as a defibrillator to bring your relationship back to life has yet to go mainstream. I think part of the problem is a lot of people don't know what the process of couples therapy actually looks like or why it works. There are also a lot of harmful myths about couples therapy floating around out there, so often, people don't know what to expect and likely fear the worst.

When I asked psychologists Simone Humphrey and Signe Simon, who run the *Lovelink* podcast together, if they've bumped up against misconceptions about what goes on in the room, they were quick to say yes. Apparently, one of the main ones that prevents people from seeking couples counseling is the belief that the therapist will take sides. People are afraid, Signe shares, that "they are going to be blamed for their behavior and it's going to be one-sided." Simone has particularly noticed this assumption in a lot of heterosexual couples. She explains that often "the male partner is really reluctant. And he's worried that both the therapist and his wife are going to gang up on him... And often what happens when they come in is that the male partner is shocked that the therapist really understands and validates his emotions. And all of a sudden he becomes more attached and excited about the therapeutic process." It then falls on the wife, in this example, to realize that she's also contributing to whatever dynamic is causing issues in their relationship. This realization can be "disorienting or disarming to both of them." Especially if the wife was expecting an ally but instead finds an impartial third party. But ultimately the initial discomfort is worth it because it allows for real progress and change.

Another major misconception, Signe says, is that the main goal of couples therapy is to keep the relationship together. Instead, Signe explains, "The goal is for two people to understand each other better, to get to a deeper level of vulnerability with each other... The outcome of that might be that they decide that they don't want to stay together." This could explain why someone who is ambivalent about their relationship might avoid couples therapy because they (incorrectly) believe they will be forced to stay. In reality, it might provide them with some much-needed clarity on whether this is the life and relationship they want.

There is also the possibility of discernment therapy, which I mentioned in Chapter Four, if one partner's foot is hovering out the door. This is a brief form of couples therapy that helps people figure out if they want to stay, go or commit to a certain period of really trying to work on things (often by attending more traditional couples therapy together). In either case, "successful" couples therapy isn't solely measured on two people staying together, but on the health and happiness of individuals.

The next major misunderstanding regarding couples therapy directly ties into my prevention-focused agenda. Couples therapy actually works best when people *aren't* in crisis. Yep! You read that right! While couples therapy can help relationships "on the brink of separation or divorce," Simone explains that it is actually most effective before things get bad. When couples are already struggling, Signe says, "there's a lot of work that needs to be done before the actual work of connecting people when a couple is in crisis. Whereas, if they're coming in for premarital or they're already in a good place, they're really committed to each other and they just want to take it to the next level. It's like the work can get really deep very quickly."

This makes sense on two levels. The first is that you are much more likely to be open and vulnerable around someone you aren't in direct conflict with. Couples therapy requires what I would like to call "extreme vulnerability." For it to work, you kind of need to lay yourself bare. And unlike in individual therapy, Simone explains, "You can't hide in couples therapy. You can't really lie" because your spouse is there to call you out on any bullshit. So if I have to be honest in session, I would personally rather bare my soul to someone I am eagerly planning a future with than with someone who has recently been a source of distress in my life. It is much easier to be vulnerable with someone who doesn't feel like a threat to your emotional safety. Plus going earlier in your relationship also means you haven't spent years or decades getting used to maladaptive patterns or cycles with each other. Simone notes that once patterns are "crystallized" or reinforced in our behavior it makes it "so much harder to untangle them." That's why the sooner, the better if you start to notice things you don't particularly like.

All this makes me wonder, how early is too early to go to couples therapy? Is it okay to pitch it as a fun and flirty fifth date idea? Or should you wait until you're at least engaged? As usual, I think it's a case-by-case basis (with very few of those cases ready for a fifth date/intake session). While it might be hard to distinguish where you fall from inside your relationship, there are going to be some couples who have more conflict or concerns from the get-go than others. Maybe you realize you want different things long-term, or you find yourself regularly fighting during what is normally considered the honeymoon phase. In those types of situations, it would be beneficial to seek counseling before making the commitment to get married or even move in together. But if you aren't dealing with a clear conflict, it can be helpful to go whenever there is going to be a big life change such as...drumroll please...getting married.

Seeking premarital counseling isn't just a good idea, it can also be an easier sell than asking your partner to go to traditional couples therapy. I've known since we started dating that I wanted to one day go to couples therapy with John to avoid, I don't know, another sudden and shocking broken engagement. (And/or make sure we are actually on the same page about life, commitment, and how many dogs I can have at one time.) But I also knew I needed to pitch the idea in a way that made sense to him. John was raised Catholic so he was familiar with the idea of Pre-Cana, which is a series of counseling sessions engaged couples have to take part in to be married in the Catholic Church. I told him that I basically wanted a nonreligious version of this once we got engaged. A few premarital sessions just to get our ducks in a row. Framing my intention with these terms and language helped make it easier for him to see the value of premarital counseling and not feel threatened or worried something was wrong. Because, like we've covered, premarital counseling doesn't mean anything is wrong. Instead, it's an opportunity to do something right ahead of time.

I've come to view going to couples therapy as a sort of emotional prenup or postnup. You are using the time to agree to the terms of how you want to treat each other over the course of your marriage while also getting a better understanding of what the other person is bringing to the relationship emotionally (instead of financially). And you have a third party in the room to make sure no one is being taken advantage of. Being proactive about couples therapy is a powerful and brave way to show your care and commitment for your partner even if other people read into it in the wrong way. Much like a prenup! (I know some of my metaphors have been a reach, but I feel like this one really tracks.)

Now that we've covered the misconceptions of couples therapy, it's time to explore the realities. What are the actual mechanisms therapists use to bring change? Because, despite what premium dramas would have you think, it's not just two people yelling at each other while a third person nods gravely with mild disappointment. There actually isn't a universal experience because different therapists use different methodologies, so when you sign up to meet with a couples therapist, it's helpful to know what techniques and philosophies they use. Some approaches are going to jive more with your personality and needs than others. Before diving into differences, though, I wanted to share the foundation that exists throughout all forms of couples therapy. And to do this I turned to Kathleen Eldridge, a clinical psychologist and researcher, to break it down for us. Here are five principles that can be found across many approaches to couples therapy:

1. Help couples understand problems more dyadically and objectively. Instead of blaming one person, you are trying to help them identify "the cycle that they're both involved in." What are they each doing, even unintentionally, to continue a problem?

2. Modify all behaviors related to safety in the relationship. This includes abuse of any kind, along with addictions such as substance use or gambling. (That said, there is a lot of debate about whether couples therapy is the right intervention when a relationship is abusive. The advice in this chapter is aimed at nonabusive relationships.)

3. Help couples feel more comfortable expressing their feelings and thoughts with each other. This is often done by first helping them individually learn how to identify and feel their own emotions and then creating a safe space for couples to have emotion-based discussions.

4. Improve communication skills. These include "skills for sharing thoughts and feelings," "skills for listening to one another" and "skills for defining and resolving specific problems."

5. Build on existing strengths. This involves "emphasizing the positives that already exist" and "intentionally increasing behaviors that are associated with satisfaction in the relationship." By focusing on strengths,

couples are able to "build a new sort of narrative about the relationship that's not entirely problem-saturated." And begin to tell themselves a better story about their relationship.

While these five goals exist throughout most couples therapy, therapists have different ways of helping couples achieve them. As much as I'd love to get into the weeds of every single modality out there, there is such a thing as too much information. So I'm going to focus on two distinct types that I find particularly appealing. The first is called Emotion Focused Couples Therapy (EFCT) and it was created by Dr. Sue Johnson. (You should hear the way people in the field talk about Dr. Sue Johnson. She's basically a rock star.) As you might guess from the name, EFCT is very focused on people's emotional truths and experiences. Both Simone and Signe specialize in EFCT, and when I asked why, Simone said that she grew up with what she felt were emotionally repressed, divorced parents so "emotion focused couples therapy was the ultimate corrective experience... I think being in a room with a couple and helping them repair and open up taps into something kind of deeper for me." Signe expressed a similar sentiment about the power of being part of emotional, experiential work versus just focusing on cognitive change or analysis.

The foundation of EFCT, Simone explains, is rooted in attachment theory. As a refresher, this is the idea that our early bonds with caretakers influence how we show up and behave in adult relationships. Simone says, "When we feel like [our] connection is threatened, we respond with different survival strategies. We get anxious, we shut down and withdraw. We avoid. And so EFCT really looks at how to kind of create security and safety in the relationship…and how to help people kind of respond to one another so that they can regulate one another." I love this because it is so simple, yet rather foreign from how many of us are brought up.

American millennials grew up with so much importance placed on the individual and individual growth that we rarely realize how much our interactions with other people contribute to our emotional state. It turns out, we can't completely control how we think and feel without taking our greater context into account—even if you meditate five times a day. Considering the impact of this outside influence on our internal state, we want to build relationships where partners are able to calm each other down instead of riling each other up. While this might seem like you are putting too much of the onus on your partner, learning how to help each other emotionally regulate isn't a sign of a codependent relationship. It's actually a sign of interdependence, which I personally find to be the sweet spot. (Interdependence is when you are dependent on another person while still able to flourish and grow on your own. Like how it was easier to go to grad school because I knew John would have dinner ready for me when I came home exhausted and occasionally annoyed that someone had flippantly said "I'm so OCD" again because they were well organized. By letting him support me, I have more capacity to help and enrich myself.)

One of the first steps of EFCT is to come to understand the interpersonal dynamics or patterns of a couple, and there are a few different archetypes that people tend to fall into (which came up briefly in Chapter Four). The first is the pursuer, who Simone describes as "the person that is really seeking connection and oftentimes feels very anxious about it. So they're the ones that are maybe getting more frustrated, reactive…getting angry, especially in the face of disconnection." Withdrawers, on the other hand, "tend to pull back, they tend to shut down, they tend to close in on themselves." Sometimes you end up with two withdrawers, sometimes you end up with two pursuers, but often a couple consists of one of each. The goal of EFCT is to identify how these roles contribute to negative cycles in the relationship. You then try to get to the emotional heart of what is causing your partner to act a certain way so you can, as Simone puts it, "create new, more positive cycles. Once you create positive cycles," she continues, "you create more connection. And things that may have been really difficult before, like problem-solving or negotiating certain things, become a lot easier because there's a lot of care and love for one another."

In order to uncover these dynamics, EFCT doesn't have people fill out attachment style quizzes or even name what style they identify with. Instead, therapists are looking for examples of the specific patterns at play. Simone will ask

clients, "What does it look like when you feel really rejected or abandoned?" She'll ask someone to go back to a
specific fight with their partner and inquire, "What was
happening in your body? What thoughts were you having?" The aim isn't to rehash a fight, but to bring the conflict alive in the therapy room so clients can work through
their emotions in real time. Properly understanding your
partner's *underlying emotions* and not just their *resulting behavior* is a cornerstone of the process.

Gaining a better understanding of yourself also makes
the process of partnership easier.

Signe says that knowing how your personal history leads
to your emotion and subsequent behavior can be "really or-
ganizing" and help relieve shame and self-criticism. It also
allows your partner to be more empathetic toward reactions
that might not make logical sense to them because they can
connect it to the larger context. Then it's easier to respond
differently in the moment and identify their partner's trigger
points for the future. "They can say 'Oh, okay, my partner is
actually being really triggered because I know their history.
Let me go and comfort them rather than, you know, yell
back at them.'" Even the language we use is important. It's
quite a different experience when you think of your partner as triggered instead of "freaking out" or "overreacting."

As you can probably tell, successful EFCT requires massive amounts of vulnerability. But you aren't just being
vulnerable for the sake of being vulnerable. The act of
being that open with a partner can be a mechanism of
change in and of itself. Simone and other EFCT therapists

help clients learn how to connect and express their raw emotions through something called enactments between partners. This is where clients turn to each other in the therapy room and share their "more vulnerable primary emotions" about the most sensitive of topics, which they likely haven't ever done before. And then you have both partners process what it's like to share [and] what it's like to receive." These kinds of deeply personal conversations allow your partner the opportunity to be there for you in a way that maybe no one else ever has been before, which builds trust and intimacy—whether the sharing is about one's childhood or a current insecurity.

Part of what makes enactments such a unique and healing experience, Simone explains, is that partners aren't just sharing their feelings in a new way, but they're also sharing their own self-concept, "their fears and what they need in the moment." Telling your partner that you fear you might be worthless or a failure or are fundamentally unlovable, only to have them respond with "no, you are worth so much" is reparative. It creates a closer connection and sense of safety within the relationship. And then, hopefully, couples are able to take this experience and replicate it outside of the therapy room and, as Signe says, shift the way you are with each other in a fundamental way. The experience in the room might also reveal that one or both partners would benefit from individual therapy as well in order to work through certain personal issues or trauma.

While I've sung the praises of couples therapy as a preventative measure, EFCT is also extremely effective following a rift or disconnection. It can even help couples come back together after an affair or onetime infidelity. (Two things that, contrary to popular belief, don't have to automatically signal the end of a relationship.) One of the things I love most about EFCT is how effective it is for people who have historically struggled to share their emotions, because unlike some of you reading this book, not everyone opens up easily, and if that's not you, maybe it's your partner. Like I've mentioned, couples therapy only works when both people are active participants and sometimes that can be difficult for a withdrawer. So a big focus of EFCT, especially when the dyad is made up of a pursuer/withdrawer, is withdrawer reengagement.

I can imagine that a lot of pursuers go into couples therapy thinking that it's the withdrawer who needs to change. It's the withdrawer who is causing all the problems by shutting down or pulling away. But something interesting EFCT often does is start by initiating changes in the pursuer, not the withdrawer. (Plot twist!) Signe explains that the therapist will validate the pursuer's experience and feelings and then try "to get them to drop down below the anger and reactivity." This is called pursuer softening. Once the pursuer is in a calmer place, it "allows the withdrawer to come forward and risk being more themselves because it's safer now." We often make the false assumption that just because someone withdraws, they aren't invested in the relationship or they don't have a lot going on below the surface. This is rarely the case. By changing tactics and softening, the pursuer is more likely to access the connection and/or information they had been hunting for in the first place. Apparently that old saying about getting more with honey than vinegar isn't just propaganda being pushed by Big Honey (or the Bible). It's actually true.

Despite where it can lead you, EFCT is a slow process, especially at the beginning. No one expects you to bare your soul to your partner in the first session and solve everything immediately. Instead, couples usually start off with a 15-minute consultation call with the therapist so everyone can decide if it feels like a good fit. Then, after the first full session, the therapist will meet with each partner individually. Signe explains that this allows people to share their family history and "talk about what their experience is like in the relationship now" without fear of offending their partner. It's also an opportunity "to help them if there's something they're having difficulty communicating to their partner." After that, couples usually meet with the therapist weekly. While Simone recommends at least six months of treatment, EFCT can technically be completed in 8-20 sessions. Once couples have a good foundation they can also decrease the frequency of sessions, stop coming to therapy all together or have booster sessions on occasion, which are as-needed tune-ups. The goal is not to be in EFCT forever. The goal is to carry what you've learned in couples therapy into the real world—as a team.

While EFCT primarily focuses on emotions, Integrative Behavioral Couple Therapy (IBCT) has two different major components: acceptance and change. Kathleen got the opportunity to research this modality early in her career and loves that this approach is based on being realistic. (Something I also find refreshing given it's become my life's mission to stop romanticizing romance.) IBCT can be broken down into these two important tenets:

1. Some problems are unsolvable.

2. These problems don't have to prevent you from having a satisfying and high-quality partnership.

Isn't that exciting?! Your introverted partner doesn't have to suddenly like large parties for your marriage to make it. And a type-A planner can figure out how to happily live with someone who likes to say things like "go with the flow." We don't have to completely change each other so that we "fit" together perfectly. Instead, we want to examine what we are willing to accept and how we can become easier to live with. And we can go to large parties with our friends instead!

IBCT also pays careful attention to the sociocultural context that might be making some issues more difficult for the couple. Kathleen explains that when analyzing relationship problems, one of the things an IBCT therapist is looking for is "external stressors." Those can look like, "racism, sexism, cisgenderism, heterosexism, disability, undocumented status, ageism, financial stress, bigotry, internalized oppression." In her therapy sessions, Kathleen welcomes all these possibilities into the conversation and sees if they're playing a role in the problem. Couples can then start to understand "the larger picture of how their relationship may reflect those larger forces, which can help them reduce the blame they have toward each other. And increase their desire to really unite so they can work together in mutual resistance against that and for liberation." This doesn't absolve partners of individual responsibility, but it does highlight how our actions are often tied to greater forces at play.

I love this social justice component of IBCT. So often we put too much onus on individual responsibility and not the systems that are affecting us. It's one thing to try to have a happy marriage in a stress-free, prejudice-free, financially secure environment. Unfortunately, that environment doesn't exist. So instead we are trying to maintain connection while also battling the realities of life in the twenty-first century. Marriages don't exist in a vacuum, and it's unfair to act as though they do. Today's generation seems increasingly more willing to admit this out loud as we have more open conversations about structures of oppression.

IBCT also makes a point to focus on the "natural differences between people" as well as the "emotional sensitivities that people have from prior life experiences." As Kathleen puts it, "every relationship is an intercultural relationship." Even if you have the same socioeconomic, ethnic, and religious background as your partner, you still come from two different cultures because you (hopefully) came from two different families. And each family unit creates its own way of seeing and being in the world. Deviations between partners are inevitable and not something to fear. The more realistic we can be about the reality of marriage, the better suited we are to nurture it.

Similar to EFCT, IBCT starts with a joint session followed by individual meetings with each partner. There is then a feedback session during which those initial sessions are reviewed and the couple works with the therapist to create a treatment plan. Kathleen explains that it's important for the couple to know what they specifically want to work on and for their treatment to be as individualized as possible. The more the therapist knows about the history and background of the clients, the easier that individualization is to accomplish. In clinical trials of IBCT, couples were allowed a maximum of 26 sessions, with 23 sessions being the average. In the real world, this treatment takes as long as it takes.

One of the big questions of IBCT is, what problems do you try to fix with behavioral change and what problems do you treat with acceptance? Unfortunately, there is no specific breakdown because it varies from couple to couple. (Annoying how that keeps happening!) Behavioral change encompasses anything from "I'll stop nagging you" to "I will help with the housework" to "I'll initiate sex more." Whatever it may be, Kathleen notes the important thing is to "move where there's motivation." You don't want to pick a behavior that you or your partner is extremely reluctant to change. Instead, you want to focus on something that maybe you both see as valuable or have been wanting to change anyway. Kathleen explains that couples often start by making a list of things they want to do to "satisfy [their] partner." I appreciate that the focus is on "what will make my partner happy" instead of "what will make my partner less annoyed." The first route makes you feel like a good partner and not just a tolerable one, which I would personally find more motivating. (I love feeling like a good partner. Especially when John claps for me, which is a fun habit I suggest cultivating in all relationships.)

According to Kathleen, it's helpful to start off the IBCT process with a focus on behavioral change, because it's possible to see those results in just a few weeks, which might increase your belief in the overall therapy process.

Beyond behavioral change, the flip side of that coin is acceptance, which can take a bit more time to foster. But once it's established, it can have long-lasting effects, which makes the initial distress worth it. Kathleen explains that acceptance is "typically helpful around some of these more difficult issues, like cultural differences, differences in preferences for intimacy, sexual behavior or issues of trust." It can also be acceptance of the specific ways you communicate or operate emotionally. For example, this approach can work well if one person has a mental health disorder that is causing conflict. Instead of expecting their partner to be magically cured, the person learns more about how the specific disorder works and how it impacts their partner and their relationship so they can be better equipped to handle it. Even something as simple as your partner being a meat eater while you are a vegan might require some acceptance work so it doesn't become a source of constant conflict.

Despite never having formally done IBCT as a couple, I can still attest to the power of embracing acceptance in your relationship. As much as John and I have in common, we also have some fundamental differences that would have made me pull my hair out when I was younger. For starters, it takes John a lot longer to make decisions than me. While I err on the side of impulsivity, he is far more cautious. This applies to both big and small decisions, including where to travel and how long it takes him to shop at Costco (roughly a day and a half). Do I find his slower speed annoying because I want to get things done, move forward and appease my anxiety by marking another thing off my to-do list? Absolutely. Just like I know he often views my hastiness as reckless (and also annoying).

When I was younger, I used to think forcing your partner to "be different" was the best and only option. But it's not productive to try to change each other, because neither one of us is "right." We simply move through the world at different speeds and with different priorities. Coming to understand that my way of doing things isn't automatically the best way for every other person has been life-changing. And it definitely makes me less obnoxious, which is an ongoing goal.

Acceptance comes easier for me when I feel more secure in myself and my relationship. I then have the capacity to adopt an objective view of my partner without taking everything personally. As you can probably tell, I am an open book, who also writes books. I tend to (over)share intimate details of my life on my podcast, social media, and Substack. My instinct is to tell everything to everyone. I've had to actively work on keeping things to myself over the years and it's still a struggle.

John is the exact opposite. His instinct is to keep things close to his chest and only share what he wants to when he wants to. When I was more insecure, this personality trait would have triggered my anxieties. I would have feared that his failure to disclose everything on command equated a lack of trust that reflects badly on me and our connection, rather than seeing it for what it was: a personality trait that often comes in handy, and also makes sense given his upbringing. Turns out, it can actually be advantageous to know how to keep your mouth shut. Once I removed myself from the equation and realized this was just a fundamental difference in how we feel comfortable operating, it became far easier to accept. And it doesn't cause issues because I no longer demand that he share everything in order to calm my own anxiety. Like when he will look at his phone, gasp, and then not tell me what is going on. (Okay, maybe that one still bugs me. But I've gotten better at waiting for an explanation.)

As you probably guessed, acceptance doesn't happen overnight. Which is why I sometimes still feel my body tense up when I ask him to "please do something when you have a chance" and that chance isn't *right away*. One of the ways IBCT accounts for this slow transition is by creating situations that allow you to increase your tolerance level. The idea is similar to exposure therapy, in that you gradually expose scenarios to each other that are typically bothersome without allowing it to end in conflict or avoidance. The goal, Kathleen says, is for partners "to begin to experience it less intensely" and to decrease their recovery time. You are also learning how to care for yourself in moments of conflict or discomfort instead of needing to find a resolution right away to feel safe. A therapist works with you to find ways to calm yourself down in the moment and make the situation more tolerable, because the more tolerable something becomes, the easier it is to accept. For example, if you have a full-blown anxiety attack every time your partner takes longer than you would like to reply to a text message, their response time is going to become a huge issue in your relationship. But if you are able to self-soothe and distract yourself, it suddenly isn't as big of a deal that they aren't always on their phone when you're apart.

IBCT is also targeted in how it approaches hurt feelings in relationships. Kathleen tries to teach couples how to focus on "the wound instead of the arrow...on the vulnerability, not the violation...how you have been hurt or harmed, instead of what has your partner done." In her eyes, this is a great way for your partner to understand the impact of their actions without feeling blamed or attacked. You are simply describing your experience as the hurt party rather than hyperfocusing on what caused that hurt. Partners can then take a step back and "see the sequence of their behaviors, [and] the behaviors between them, more objectively and dyadically." This approach also helps to avoid defensiveness, because it supports the conceptualization of problems as a cycle of behaviors and not solely as one person's fault. (Again, this only applies to nonabusive relationships.)

One of the things I appreciate most about this modality is how all the different elements work together. You aren't solely focusing on behavior change and then acceptance or acceptance and then behavior change. It all interweaves at a pace tailored to the couple. You get to decide what behaviors you want to try to change and what you want to work on accepting.

You also get to decide if there are certain behaviors you don't want to accept. IBCT might help you realize that your partner isn't able (or willing) to change in the way you had been hoping or expecting. Once you have that knowledge, you then have to figure out if the relationship you currently have is enough for you. Working on acceptance doesn't mean you can't have deal-breakers, even if your deal-breakers have changed with time. Kathleen makes a point to note that maybe the end of the relationship will actually be better for an individual's well-being. And individual well-being is just as important as the well-being of your relationship (if not more so). The process of IBCT helps you get a better sense of the reality of your marriage or relationship. It exposes your differences and conflict areas and asks, "can you handle this?" while also giving you some tools to do so. You can lead a couple to water, but you can't make them drink (or fight for a marriage they no longer want).

The Gottman Institute, which is one of the leading researchers on couples, has found that the average couple waits around six years before seeking therapy to deal with their marital problems. Which begs the question, are most couples seeking help too late? Is there a moment in time when a marriage becomes too far gone for couples therapy to have a sizable impact? And if so, how can we know if our relationship is salvageable or not before baring our souls and our credit cards?

When I asked Kathleen this question, she said one of the signs that a relationship might have run its course is when one or both partners have disengaged from trying. Intense conflict can actually be more promising than passive resignation because being upset or angry means you still care. The key, Kathleen says, is to come in when both partners are still motivated and willing to make changes. If that's the case, "the prognosis is very good."

Simone felt similarly. She said she often uses fire as a metaphor to assess a couple's future. "If there're embers, there's something to work with. It doesn't have to be a full flame, but if there's some sort of willingness, if there's some sort of spark, if it feels alive in some way, I think any couple has the capacity to heal. However, if it's like cinders, if it's ash, if one partner is just totally burnt out and done, they're not going to be open to this process."

Simone also believes that in order for couples therapy

to be effective, there had to be something fundamental to begin with. If two people never really loved each other or never had a deep connection, "it's hard to create something that was never there."

Personally, I also imagine it can be difficult if two people's perceptions of marriage are profoundly different. Some people, for a variety of reasons, don't have high expectations for marriage. So when the reality of marriage isn't that fulfilling, it's not something they identify as a problem worth putting much effort into because they assume marriage isn't that fulfilling. It's just something you do when you become an adult. Other people, though, expect a certain level of connection and harmony for a marriage to continue. You can see how if those two different types of people married each other, they could hit a crossroads rather quickly. That's why seeing a couples therapist before you get married can help ensure you have similar enough expectations and the same level of work ethic when it comes to maintaining the relationship. You don't want to find yourself in a situation where you are the only one doing the (emotional) heavy lifting, while your partner is completely checked out and uninterested in helping. Even if it is painful to realize you already love someone who doesn't plan to try.

For some couples, one round of premarital counseling might be enough to get them through a lifetime together. (And if so, congratulations!) But for a lot of people, it can be helpful and even necessary to have booster sessions throughout the years. Booster sessions can help you navigate major life transitions such as having your first child, major medical issues or retirement.

While this might sound like more work (and money) than you expected, consider this: we already go for checkups at the dentist and have yearly physicals. "Why not take care of our marriage in the same way that we take care of other aspects of our health?" Kathleen asks. Especially since research seems to support that the quality of one's marriage directly impacts people's physical and mental health. The National Institute of Aging has found that the stress of a bad marriage can potentially put you at higher risk for poorer cardiovascular health—especially if you are a woman. So attending to the quality of your relationship isn't the kind of thing you can safely put on the back burner. Marriage is one of the hardest things you can do, and yet there is an expectation that if it doesn't come naturally, it is rotten or flawed.

This harmful perception can then prevent people from being proactive about marriage maintenance because we don't assume every marriage can benefit from it. We falsely believe that only *some* people need to spend extra time "fixing things" or "reconnecting" when we *all* need to make space to regularly attend to the health of our marriages. It should be just as much of a weekly priority as eating nutritious foods or getting our heart rates up. Embracing marriage as an area of life that needs consistent tending will help make stronger, healthier marriages, and in turn make stronger, healthier individuals. Not to mention, it's easier for us to seek outside help when we anticipate needing it.

And now for my rant.

Couples therapy is rarely covered by insurance because, as The Couples Center, a large organization throughout California, explains, it is not considered to be "medically necessary." In order for individual therapy to be covered by insurance, there needs to be a medical diagnosis. (Which is why so many people have the code for Generalized Anxiety Disorder on their bill. It's the least potentially stigmatizing disorder to have on your record.) So, while there might be some cases where a therapist is able to convince an insurance company that one partner's disorder is being treated through couples therapy, it is not a likely outcome. All this means that while couples therapy is an incredible and effective resource, it is currently available only to people who can afford to pay out of pocket.

This socioeconomic divide is part of what adds to marriage being a class issue. Wealthy couples don't just have a better chance of getting married in the first place, they have a better chance of maintaining and building a healthy marriage because they can pay for professional help. They are also more likely to have time to work on their marriage because they probably aren't juggling multiple jobs or consumed with thinking about how to pay for their groceries. So if you're in the financial position to go to couples therapy, don't think of it as an obligation or a drag. Think of it as a privilege and tremendous opportunity to prioritize one of the most important relationships in your life.

Although couples therapy is the gold standard for helping your relationship, there are other more affordable resources out there until we can revolutionize the health care system. (Including what you are reading right now!) If you find yourself wanting some additional support or guidance, you can check out the resources section in the back of the book.

But for now, since you are already here, why not start off with the following:

QUESTIONS TO ASK YOURSELF:

- Do I have a negative association with couples therapy? If so, why? And is it serving me?
- What can I do to make difficult situations with my partner more tolerable? How can I better care for myself during moments of distress or disconnection? (For example, deep breathing, going for a long walk or remembering to eat.)
- Have my deal-breakers changed with time? What are they now?
- Does being vulnerable with my partner make me uncomfortable? If so, is this something I want to work on by opening myself up more and getting used to increased intimacy?

QUESTIONS TO ASK YOUR PARTNER:

- What are our expectations for a healthy and fulfilling marriage? Do we need a certain level of mutual satisfaction to keep it going?

- In what way might our different cultures and backgrounds lead to conflict?
- What are the main outside stressors in our relationship and how can we work together to deal with them?
- Are there any behavioral changes we are motivated to make to be better partners to each other?
- What would it look like to embrace more acceptance in our relationship? What do you wish I would grow to accept about you and vice versa?

Congratulations! You made it through my pro-couples-therapy campaign! I don't know if I changed any of your minds, but I do know you'll want to keep reading because the sex chapter is next. And it might just blow your socks off! (Unless you prefer to keep them on! No judgment.)

8
FORSAKING ALL OTHERS

Keeping Your (Sexual) Spark Alive

The fastest way to ruin your sex life is to get married.

Or so pop culture (and a lot of stand-up comics) would have you believe. As much as society pushes for people to legally couple up, there is an undercurrent that doing so will have very negative repercussions in the bedroom. So do you really have to give up sex in order to share health insurance? No siree bob! There are actually no definitive studies that prove single people have more sex than married people—and even a couple suggest the opposite.

But quantity is not the same as quality. Getting married doesn't mean you can check "having a satisfying sex life" off your to-do list and forget about it. Like most things, maintaining a sexual spark takes work. There's even a popular belief in the mental health field that when your sex life is good, it only constitutes about 10% of the relationship. But if your sex life is a problem, it suddenly becomes front and center of everything. This makes sense to me, because we as a society put *so* much pressure on the importance of sex in romantic relationships that when even one thing goes awry, it can feel catastrophic. So to avoid this issue taking over our lives, we often have to carry the work into the bedroom too. Even if it's easier to pretend everything is fine and keep rewatching *New Girl* until you pass out (like me).

Given the big role sex can play in the overall well-being of your relationship, it's understandable that married sex can easily become a source of anxiety. While it might not seem like that big of a deal to have the same roommate for the rest of your life, it can feel existentially overwhelming when you think about only having one sex partner until you die (if you've agreed to be monogamous). Even if you're open or polyamorous, is it really possible to stay attracted to the same person decade after decade as you grow older together? Especially if you spend the majority of your time raising kids and acting like best friends instead of lovers? And what the heck are you supposed to do if you have different sex drives? Give up? Flip a coin?! Heads you leave me alone, tails we bang?

Thankfully, the sex therapists I've interviewed for this chapter shared some ways they help clients navigate the most common concerns so we can learn how to make married sex a source of connection and not tension.

Part of what makes it difficult to seamlessly slide into matrimonial bliss under the bedsheets is that we aren't conditioned in modern American culture to have healthy or accurate conceptions about sex. As an intersectional feminist who has been a practicing sex-positive psychologist for more than 20 years, Dr. Nikki Coleman knows this firsthand. She has seen how societal messaging about sex, shame and gender have hurt people's abilities to go into marriages with a realistic idea of what to expect. Dr. Nikki explains, "The crazy part about our gender socialization is, it doesn't matter what your sexual orientation is, we all get fed the same stuff." And that stuff is that sex is a dirty bad thing. But also somehow extremely important? You can see why we are all set up to fail a bit in this arena. Even with the rise of the sex positivity movement over recent decades, there is still a lot to unlearn for millennials and Gen Z alike.

Dr. Nikki explains that regardless of how secular your current life is, "religious shame still has a lot of influence on our expectations about sex." But even outside of religion, women or people socialized as female "get a lot of messages about how to be a good girl or good wife with regard to limiting sexual contact premaritally but once you get married, you're supposed to be like a porn star." There is also a lot of pressure for women to remain attractive in heterosexual relationships along with a societal focus on "women's abilities to please their man." Meanwhile, far less attention is given to women's access to pleasure or how couples can cocreate pleasure together. This type of messaging is so prevalent it affects people even if they don't buy into organized religion or the gender binary.

All of this historical baggage (and bullshit) often results in people having to actively unpack their preconceptions about what a fulfilling sex life actually looks like in order to have one. Through no fault of your own, you, yes you, might be holding on to harmful beliefs about sex without even realizing it. Dr. Catalina Lawsin, a clinical psychologist and researcher, believes many people fall into the trap of thinking that if our partner truly loves us, "they know exactly what pleases us. That they know when we need it, how we need it... And that if they don't, they don't love us enough, period." This is just one of many assumptions that gets in the way of figuring out how to be good sexual partners to each other through communication and time. And not just magical mind reading abilities.

Michelle Herzog, a certified sex therapist and marriage and family therapist, who founded The Center for Modern Relationships in Chicago, also pointed out the popular but false belief that both partners *have* to orgasm for the sex to be good. Considering the wide range of reasons that people have difficulty orgasming or an inability to, categorizing sex in this way can lead to unnecessary judgment and shame. Orgasm-less sex can still bring connection, fun, and pleasure. (And I will die on this hill.) Another harmful assumption is that "real" sex is penetrative. This is not only untrue but painfully heteronormative. "Real" sex is whatever you want it to be! I'll admit that it's easy to read this and see the flawed logic when it's spelled out in front of you, but plenty of people never take the time to realize what they might consciously or subconsciously be buying into. That's why I'm forcing us all to take that time right now.

Personally, I think one of the hardest ingrained beliefs to push back against is the idea that it is your partner's responsibility to remain attractive to you instead of seeing it as your responsibility to maintain your attraction to them. Let me break that down further in case you vehemently disagree and were about to give up on me. As a disclaimer, I don't think you are solely responsible for feeling passionate or sexual toward your partner in all circumstances, regardless of what they do or how they treat you. But I do think we're quick to place the entire onus on the other person to ignite those feelings in us, instead of examining what we can do to flame our desire toward our partner. Because one of the realities of married life is that you will inevitably see your partner doing things that directly conflict with your notion of them as an always-gorgeous, mysterious, all-powerful sexual being. You will see them when they are tired and cranky. You will smell them when they eat too much dairy and have gas. You will likely wash their dirty underwear more often than you will rip it off in the heat of passion. In those moments, it can feel like the person you once couldn't keep your hands off of no longer exists. But, as Dr. Nikki points out, the person hasn't changed—your perception of them has.

We have to acknowledge that it is normal to not always

feel the same level of passion for your partner. Context matters and it's unlikely that you're going to want to jump your partner's bones right after getting into an argument about how to correctly load the dishwasher. What is possible, however, is to make a conscious effort to diversify the contexts in which we see our partners. Maybe you think they have a sexy singing voice, so you purposefully plan a karaoke session. Maybe you love seeing them take control of a room, so you have them practice their work presentation in front of you after the kids have gone to bed. It can be helpful to remind ourselves of the parts of them that we have historically been sexually drawn to, and we can give ourselves opportunities to reawaken those old perceptions in real time instead of relying on memories to get you through. That's why I keep asking John to act out entire scenes of *I Think You Should Leave* because his Tim Robinson impression is so spot on. (What can I say? Laughter is an aphrodisiac!)

I also think there is an expectation in Western culture that sexual desire should come frequently. This line of thinking not only erases asexual people's experiences, but can make allosexual people feel broken if they have a hard time tapping into that side of themselves. (Allosexual is an umbrella term for anyone who doesn't identify as asexual and experiences some form of sexual attraction.)

Michelle says that one of the most common things she sees as a sex therapist is a couple trying to navigate a desire discrepancy, which is when one partner wants to be sexually intimate more often than the other. This can cause problems because the partner with the "higher sex drive" might feel like they are constantly being rejected (I used quotes for reasons that will soon become clear). While the partner with the "lower sex drive" often thinks there is something wrong with themselves that they need to fix. It's obvious why this kind of dynamic can be a source of strain for everyone. And why sexual problems can easily overtake your entire relationship.

I think a little reframing and psychoeducation can go a long way for couples who struggle in this arena. For starters, Dr. Nikki is quick to point out that the idea of a "high" or "low" sex drive might not even be the right way to look at it. You don't have a certain fixed amount of desire that you have to parcel out over the course of your life. Things can either activate or deactivate your ability to become aroused. Dr. Nikki explains that "partners in the couple probably have comparable desire for sex over-all, but the ability to get to the place of wanting to be aroused can get cluttered in different ways over time." So it can end up seeming like one person simply isn't as interested when really there are just more barriers in their way, while their partner, on the other hand, is able to access arousal more easily.

These barriers to arousal can take a lot of different forms. For example, "Do I feel sexy? Do I feel good in my body? Do I feel wanted by my partner? Do I have enough energy at the end of the day to direct toward this sexual experience?" If the answer to any of those questions is no, it can start to feel like sex is a chore and not something you actually want. It's easy to then make the leap that you have a fixed "low" sex drive if you don't understand what is actually getting in your way of your desire.

Part of what can make defining sex drives extra tricky is that people can have totally different relationships to sex. For some, sex is a way to relieve stress. For others, having sex while stressed is the last thing they want to do. There are also distinct differences in the way people experience desire. Some feel spontaneous desire, meaning there isn't a direct cause. It basically pops out of nowhere and suddenly you're just ready to go. But for those who have a more responsive type of desire, something has to activate it, such as quality time spent together and/or a sensual foot massage. Yet, this extra step might be foreign to a partner who regularly experiences spontaneous desire. So learning that responsive desire exists and how it works can be extremely useful for a spontaneous partner who assumes a wink and a nudge should be enough to seal the deal.

Once everyone understands how responsive desire works, it's easier to activate it. Michelle helps couples learn "how to cultivate situations in which the body feels really good, or how to cultivate situations in which one partner feels emotionally connected to the other because that's what they need in order to feel sexual." It's not that a person with responsive desire isn't attracted to their partner or uninterested in having sex. They just need to get to a place where their body and mind are ready and eager for that kind of interaction.

Michelle adds, "A major part of working on differing

desires is being intentional. When both partners in the relationship are actively engaged and willing to work on sexual fulfillment, they can see significant changes in their sex lives as a couple. But if needs aren't being met within the relationship, sharing the responsibility of cultivating a pleasurable and fulfilling sex life may be challenging." Basically, if you aren't showing up for your partner outside of the bedroom, it's going to be harder to improve your sex life consistently and holistically.

But what does "improvement" actually mean? I mentioned earlier that quality matters more than quantity. Except, not everyone thinks that way. It's much easier to count how frequently you're making whoopee than to do a deep dive into how emotionally and sexually fulfilling each individual session was (or wasn't). Even when we talk with our friends about sex, the first question is normally, "How often do you do it" not "when you do do it, is it satisfying?" This all feeds into the false belief that frequent sex is what keeps couples together, so we focus on hitting a quota instead of cultivating a fulfilling sex life. This numbers-focused mindset can then lead to an unhealthy sense of obligation. Dr. Nikki has seen many clients, especially women or people socialized as women, feel enormous amounts of pressure to maintain their marriage through frequent sex. There is a widespread fear that if you don't please your partner enough they will find that pleasure from someone else or leave you (or both!).

While Dr. Nikki won't "discredit the reality of that threat," she does go on to say, "it's wholly unfair that one person is responsible for keeping the relationship alive based on one aspect of the relationship." As someone who has been conditioned to put these unfair expectations on myself, it felt like a sigh of relief to hear her break it down in this way. One of my greatest fears has always been that if I don't find a way to rally at a frequent enough pace, everything will fall apart and it'll be all my fault. But now I'm realizing that looking at sex in this transactional way isn't just harmful to me, it's harmful to the relationship. Sex is a part of our connection to another person. It is not a required payment for someone being a supportive partner. (I tell myself again and again and...again.)

That said, what happens outside the bedroom does have a big impact on people's sex life without people realizing it. Dr. Nikki will often tell straight men, "You want more sex? Then you need to do more to make it easier" for her to have it. You might think making things "easier" means lighting some candles and activating your partner's responsive desire. But Dr. Nicki is talking about more than that. As much as we want to believe in egalitarian relationships, the household mundanity of life often falls unevenly on women (like we discussed in Chapter One) so it can then become a challenge for a female spouse to make space for sex in her life. One way to combat this, as her partner, is to take on more domestic work so your wife has less on her plate. Obviously this is in reference to heterosexual relationships, but I think the distribution of domestic work is imperfect in any marriage. If one partner is tasked with getting dinner ready, cleaning up and putting the kids to bed, it's unlikely they will have the energy to do much of anything at the end of the day other than zone out and pray for the sweet release of sleep. While bringing home flowers or sending sexy texts are more explicitly "romantic," what might really help someone get in the mood is having fewer responsibilities. Especially if they run anxious and have a hard time letting go when there is a looming to-do list in their mind. (Yes, I am talking about me.)

Cultivating and maintaining a fulfilling sex life with your spouse is a tricky goal because it requires both teamwork and individual responsibility. Michelle explains, "I truly believe that each person is responsible for their own sexual part and their own sexual self." But that doesn't mean you have to address your issues in secret. It's important to share any problems that one partner may be having with the other, because chances are that partner can already feel a disconnection. If these are new issues, you want to be curious about what is happening with you and/or your sexual relationship and—here's the hardest part—openly talk about it. Dr. Nikki says, "healthy couples are able to sort of turn in and say, 'Okay, this thing that I'm struggling with is now affecting both of us. Let me be accountable for that thing and also let me let you support me in this thing.' It's not an either/or it's a both/and." This balance of personal responsibility while still accepting help from our partners is basically the backbone of any successful partnership. Adding more "both/and" into our lives helps us maintain our individuality while reaping the benefits of having a spouse in the first place. And it's especially useful to lean on your partner's support when dealing with something that might otherwise be a source of shame or self-judgment, like sexual dysfunction.

Fatima, a first-generation Palestinian American, grew up with the assumption that while men can have sex before marriage, women can't. Or, perhaps more accurately, a woman can't have premarital sex without it ruining her life and reputation. Fatima knew this was an unfair double standard since Islam forbids sex before marriage for everyone, but culturally, she says, it was the reality she lived in. This ideological climate also led her to believe that women should be passive when it came to romantic relationships. She thought she needed to wait around for her future husband to find her. But by the time she reached 27, she realized she needed to be more proactive in this area of her life if she wanted to get married. So, after working with a therapist, she got to a place where she felt comfortable signing up for a Muslim dating app and putting herself out there. One of her well-respected female cousins had recently found her spouse using the same app, which made this otherwise unseemly approach more palatable.

When Fatima matched with Nasir, she was surprised to find he was waiting for marriage to have sex too. He was from a more Western family and, while he was raised Muslim, his mixed-race mother never converted to the religion. He lived a more secular lifestyle and even felt comfortable openly telling his now divorced parents he had a girlfriend. (Meanwhile, Fatima didn't mention his existence to her parents until Nasir was ready to propose.) But it turned out that despite his less conservative up- bringing, Nasir had the same values around sex as Fatima, which was a huge relief for her. They were going to get to explore this massive thing together.

While Fatima might have been a virgin when she got married, that doesn't mean she escaped societal messag- ing around sex. Sex was everywhere, and she was ex- cited to finally join in on the fun. She expected her first experience to maybe be a little awkward, but ultimately satisfying and easy. That didn't happen. Fatima's early ex- periences with penetration were filled with vaginal pain, which was something she hadn't anticipated. She had wor- ried she might feel "dirty" for no longer being pure or be embarrassed showing her naked body to her husband. But neither of those things turned out to be issues. In- stead, she was confronted with a heartbreaking truth: sex felt nothing like she thought it would. She vacillated be- tween feeling cheated and feeling broken. She had waited years to experience the thing everyone couldn't stop talk- ing about, only to find it, well, awful.

To make matters more complicated, Nasir's body wasn't having the same reaction. For him, sex was easy and satis- fying. In some relationships, this type of disconnect could drive people apart. And Fatima was afraid it might hap- pen to them. She was not only worried that something might be physically wrong with her, she feared she was ruining sex for her new husband. In a moment of insecurity, she even declared that Nasir should find himself a new wife. Nasir, however, never got angry or disappointed that Fatima wasn't having the time of her life in bed. He never blamed her for her difficulties and was determined to work through the issue as a team. For him, the end goal wasn't just to make sex less painful for his wife so they could have it more often, but to find a way to make it actually enjoyable—which is an important distinction.

Luckily, despite her disappointment, Fatima didn't avoid the issue or hope it would magically get better with time and nothing else. Her regular therapist referred her to a sex therapist, and Fatima dove in headfirst: she was actually so open and honest during those first few phone sessions that her sex therapist thanked her for her transparency. Fatima initially found this funny—what was the point of hiring a sex therapist if she wasn't going to share every single detail? She later realized she was only able to be so open about a rather taboo subject because 1) she'd already gotten used to sharing intimate details with her regular therapist and 2) sex therapy is expensive and she wanted to make sure she got a bang for her buck. Plus by the time she connected with him, she was desperate to talk about her struggles with a neutral third party. She was ready to try anything.

Fatima's sex therapist quickly got to work by providing actionable steps to change her relationship with sex. Fatima realized that, in order for sex to be pleasurable for both partners, she needed to figure out how to approach it in a calmer fashion since her nerves had a tendency to take over and make everything worse. Her therapist worked with her on deep breathing, and she started to take deep breaths and meaningful pauses leading up to and during intercourse. She also examined her daily routine and realized that she was too tired at night, so focusing on sex in the morning or afternoon was a better and more productive approach. Fatima learned that it is okay to need additional help and would sometimes take Advil for the pain (although pain during intercourse may necessitate further consultation with a doctor to rule out physical causes). Of everything she tried, the deep breathing was the most effective. Instead of feeling tense and terrified, engaging in calming breaths allowed her to be more open and relaxed, helping alleviate her physical pain. She also realized that vaginal penetration isn't the only way to be sexually intimate, which was an emotional relief. There was more to physically explore than she had been led to believe.

Throughout her time in sex therapy, Fatima included Nasir in her process and progress. She started to openly communicate what she needed from him in the moment and what she needed from him long-term. He was happy to try different things and be flexible, which probably made all that direct communication less scary. While Fatima still thinks that sex is "overhyped," it is no longer a strain on their relationship. She is able to enjoy the intimacy and connection that comes with it, even if her physical reaction isn't what she once thought it might be. Sex is now a special part of her life that she shares with her husband, which is meaningful in itself. Fatima's sex therapist told her early on in their work together that it is a great thing she is married because it means they are in it for the long haul. They have time to figure it all out. This sentiment stuck with her and gave her hope. They weren't doomed. They were just starting.

So much of our anxiety and fear around "mating for life" can likely be traced back to having unrealistic expectations. One of which is that our relationship to sex should stay the same as we age, and if it doesn't, we will be unsatisfied and unhappy. But bodies change and many of us will probably deal with chronic illness or disability as we get older (if we aren't already). These types of changes, along with general aging, are going to have an impact on our ability or willingness to be sexual.

To make matters even more complicated, it won't just be our bodies that inevitably change with time: so will our minds. Michelle explains that mental shifts can influence "what we're attracted to and what we're not…what we like and what we don't like. These things will shift over time, as well as our desire." So if all this change is likely coming, but we can't control or predict it, how do we not spiral or expect the worst? I've found it helps to simply have a flexible mindset. If we *expect* change, it lessens the blow. Being flexible also encourages us to be more open to explore new ways to feel sexually fulfilled and connected outside of our standard routine. Not all change has to be bad. Change can even be…neutral! (Shocking, I know.)

According to Dr. Catalina, it's important to normalize shifts in your sexual relationship. You don't want to pathologize. You want to investigate. She asks, "What were the factors that contributed to this shift? What was happening in the relationship that fostered this shift?" Maybe you are having a hard time feeling desirable in your body after giving birth. Maybe you are mentally exhausted after being in a pandemic. Maybe your in-laws moved into your guest room and the walls are thin. Being able to name a reason behind the changes can help contextualize the decline in your sex life, and prevents you from jumping to the conclusion that the *magic is gone forever* before passively falling into the trap of assuming this is your new normal.

If having a fulfilling sex life is a priority for you and your partner—which isn't the case for everyone—you have to find ways to make it a priority. Many experts believe that focusing on self-pleasure can be an effective place to start. As Michelle points out, it's unrealistic to expect our partner to always be sexually available at the same exact time we want to be sexual. When we feel aroused but our partner isn't in the same headspace, self-pleasure is an adaptive and positive option. But if you aren't craving a release so much as a connection, you can always suggest other ways to be intimate that aren't explicitly sexual, like something as simple as cuddling. She teaches couples to use the following statement when they find themselves in this type of dynamic: "I don't feel like I can show up for that right now, but I can do (fill in the blank with what you are able and willing to show up for instead).” That fill-in-the-blank can be a wide range of other activities that are more aligned with both partners current state of mind, and it prevents the initiator from feeling rejected.

But the *fear* of getting rejected is not something that should be overlooked. It's useful to learn these tips and tricks for bumps in the road, but they don't necessarily wipe out an underlying worry that your spouse might find you less attractive as you age. I certainly think about this possibility a lot, which makes sense given our youth-obsessed culture and the total erasure of most women over fifty (aside from Helen Mirren). As Dr. Nikki puts it, “you have to fight to have a good body image in this culture.” And sometimes we have days or months or even years where we lose that battle. But one thing that can help sustain the fight is providing your partner with a lot of positive affirmations.

Dr. Nikki often tells partners, “Whatever volume of interest and attraction or compliments they think they need to demonstrate…multiply that. It ain't enough.” This makes sense when you take into account humans' negativity bias and the “amount of garbage” all people, regardless of their gender, have internalized about their bodies over the years. You might think your partner knows you are attracted to them because you, you know, married them. But the mind is a master at making us question ourselves and our worth. Taking the time to reiterate your feelings of attraction over (and over) again can go a long way in helping your partner feel good in their body. It also dims the fear that you are losing interest.

When it comes to aging, Michelle says it's important to remind ourselves that humans don't have a "sexual expiration." There is no "age police" out there making sure octogenarians aren't getting frisky. And just because your 80-year-old grandparents seem sexless *to you* doesn't mean they feel that way about each other. If you are physically able, the decision to keep having sex as you age is entirely your own. Plenty of studies show that a significant percentage of people continue to have sex into their nineties. So assuming your sex life will end years before you die isn't just inaccurate, it's disheartening. That said, if you find that over time you and your spouse prefer a rousing game of gin rummy over a bedroom tryst, that's perfectly okay too. Sex is only one form of connection.

If there was such a thing as an anti-marriage lobby, their biggest talking point would probably be, "Do you really want to have sex with only ONE person for the REST OF YOUR LIFE?" And for some monogamous people, this probably ranks as their biggest concern when deciding whether to walk down the aisle. Is it really possible to commit to one person for a lifetime without growing restless and/or feeling compelled to cheat? I'll admit that as someone who is only comfortable being sexual in a committed relationship, I've never worried about having only one partner. In fact, it feels like a relief. But I have feared my partner would want to stray or, even worse, feel trapped. Given all the old ball-and-chain messaging out there, it's hard not to think that way. And with more and more couples openly trying nonmonogamy, it begs the question, are we set up to fail when it comes to monogamy? Is it completely counterintuitive to human nature?

I don't think so. But I'm monogamous! And it's worth pointing out that marriage and monogamy do not have to be one and the same. There are lots of married couples who practice ethical nonmonogamy. If you're not familiar with this setup, think of nonmonogamy as an umbrella term that can describe a wide variety of sexual arrangements. Some couples might only agree to casual hookups with strangers, while others identify as polyamorous and have full-blown committed relationships with other people. Under ethical nonmonogamy, each individual couple makes its own rules for what type of arrangement works best for them.

In an ideal world, we would all have taken the time to question whether monogamy is actually right for us before entering into a serious relationship. And maybe that can be (and is already becoming) the case for newer generations, who are more informed about their options from the start. But if you find yourself monogamously married, engaged, or seriously dating and you're suddenly curious about opening things, Dr. Nikki believes the first step is getting to the heart of what's really going on: specifically, what is appealing about opening up your relationship? If the motivation is "rooted in a sense of fear and anxiety about your desirableness...that's stuff you should probably work out in therapy." Basically, becoming nonmonogamous shouldn't be to prove your own attractiveness. It also shouldn't be to try to save your marriage or keep your partner from cheating on you by letting them openly sleep with other people. These types of approaches aren't based in a true interest in the lifestyle, but are being done out of fear of being left or hurt. However, if you realize that "you have a worldview about connecting and intimacy and relationships that is more lent to nonmonogamy" that is not something you can really ignore or keep from your partner because it is a part of your values. But you shouldn't expect it to be an easy conversation.

It might be challenging for us monogamous folk to not take the idea of seeing other people as an insult or rejection because, for us, one partner is enough to meet our sexual needs. So when the idea is initially introduced, Dr. Nikki says, "the immediate first place you go to is, 'Somebody's replacing me.'" But nonmonogomous and polyamorous people don't see it that way because "they can have multiple attachments that are intimate, affirming...and even sexual." None of which has to change how they feel about their original partner, because interest in someone new doesn't result in less interest in their spouse.

While this makes sense on a logical level, it's likely going to take time for a traditionally monogamous partner to get used to this concept since it is pretty antithetical to what we have been taught about romantic love and connection. You know all that stuff about soulmates and finding "the one." That's why, if you're in a monogamous relationship, you can't just say, "Hey, I want to open things up, and if you love me, you'll let us do that." You have to give your partner space and time to digest what you are saying, to "sit in the discomfort" of them deciding how they want to move forward. This isn't the sort of decision that should be made lightly, whether the conversation is happening before marriage or in the middle of it. (Unless you both have been secretly wanting to open things up, in which case it might just be a cause for celebration!)

When initiating this type of conversation, it shouldn't sound like an ultimatum. *You either have to let me sleep with my coworker or you lose me forever!* Instead, I imagine it's more productive to think of it like starting a negotiation. Dr. Nikki says that people often "have this false expectation that their partner is either going to accept [nonmonogamy] wholesale or reject it" but "opening it up can look a variety of different ways." These ways may include: you can only date other people as a couple. You have specific guidelines for who you are allowed to bring into the relationship. You keep things purely sexual and don't allow other emotional connections. There is a surprisingly wide spectrum between full-blown *we won't even admit we think celebrities are hot* monogamy and *we live on a commune with 10 different partners* polyamory.

In a dialogue like this, you might find that you and your partner aren't as far apart on that spectrum as you feared. Or you might realize you want two conflicting things, which is better to find out sooner than later. What you don't want to do is keep your curiosity to yourself and then resent your partner for something they didn't even know was an issue until you've already been married for a decade.

Even if you've already been married for a decade and have never discussed being open before, the same principles apply: you're allowed to explore breaking your current relationship contract of monogamy and starting a new one. You don't have to bury that part of yourself because it's not how you originally presented yourself to your partner. It's also hard to know if nonmonogamy is right for you if you've never had the chance to try it. So if you are curious, start the conversation with your spouse—just make sure to do so with a lot of forethought and empathy. As Michelle says, "It can be very surprising and confusing to a partner who signed up for monogamy to hear that their partner is all of a sudden questioning that. Because what it can start to feel like is, 'I'm not good enough. What did I do?... Was I lied to? I feel manipulated." That's why it's important to hear each other out and then decide as a unit how to move forward as a couple or—if you really can't agree on the terms and it continues to be a consistent conflict—perhaps as individuals who tried their best to make it work.

When Charlotte first met Oliver in her early twenties, she wasn't thinking about nonmonogamy. She was too focused on getting married and feeling settled. As someone with anxiety, she figured being in an exclusive commitment with someone would make her feel safe. Oliver was happy to oblige, even if it took them a bit longer to make it down the aisle than Charlotte would have liked. (They were still married by age 27. Respect for the hustle.) Oliver was everything Charlotte had ever wanted in a partner. But seven years into their marriage, Charlotte found herself wondering if they should open things up.

Charlotte's motivation for trying nonmonogamy was complicated. Part of her desire came from finally being more in touch with her body than ever before. Now in her thirties, she was in her sexual prime and had recently started weightlifting. The combo made her "revved up" and eager for new sexual connections. She also found herself craving more connection and community. But on top of all the good stuff, Charlotte was also battling insecurity and abandonment issues. While she wasn't aware of it at the time, looking back, she thinks her desire to open her marriage might have been a way to mitigate her fears of people leaving. If she had multiple romantic connections, it was less likely she would be left all alone. Or so her subconscious led her to believe.

On paper, Charlotte didn't have any tangible reasons to fear this outcome. Oliver was a committed and loving husband, and the stability she felt in her relationship with him was part of what made her feel comfortable broaching the subject of polyamory in the first place. (Which might seem counterintuitive with her fear of abandonment but, hey, humans are complicated!) The day she finally told Oliver about her new desire, she was so terrified she could barely get the words out. Oliver was shocked, but he took it in stride. He could see that this was something his wife genuinely wanted to try, so he was willing to figure out a way to make it work. They agreed to shift into polyamory while prioritizing and maintaining their marriage. But things didn't go as planned.

Charlotte had opened her marriage with the hope of forming meaningful connections with other people only to realize that those types of relationships were harder to find than she had expected. She went into the new agreement with a particular crush in mind, but their connection never panned out. And it turned out that once prospective men learned she was married, most of them were only interested in a casual sexual relationship even though she was looking for an emotional one. This was partly due to her trying to date monogamous, single people who didn't fully grasp the lifestyle instead of looking for other polyamorous partners. But moreover, dating is hard and time-consuming and she was already busy working three different jobs. She didn't have the energy (or even knowledge) to go look in better places. Oliver, on the other hand, was having a completely different experience. He had no trouble finding women who wanted to seriously date him despite him having a wife.

So it went on like this for about four years, with Oliver having all the luck and Charlotte struggling, until Oliver had a girlfriend who wanted more from him. Neither Charlotte nor his girlfriend were happy with the current balance of their relationship with Oliver, and it didn't seem sustainable. So Charlotte broached the subject of closing their marriage (again). Her experience of polyamory hadn't brought her the fulfillment she had been looking for and, if she was being totally honest, Oliver having more success was a blow to her ego. Oliver, who had tried polyamory only on her suggestion, was happy to renegotiate the terms of their marriage. They decided that full-blown relationships with other people didn't seem to work. So they came to a happy medium that has ebbed and flowed in the years since. They now fall under the umbrella of nonmonogamy, where they aren't strictly monogamous but rarely hook up with other people.

While Charlotte's foray into polyamory didn't have the intended outcome, it did change things for the better. By opening up her marriage, Charlotte was able to see that nothing, not even other lovers or girlfriends, was able to change Oliver's commitment to her. She remained his priority throughout. (Not all polyamory operates with a hierarchical structure and a primary partner, but theirs did.) The experience also brought them closer together because they had to have a lot of difficult and vulnerable conversations that might otherwise have been avoidable. Charlotte even partially credits the institution of marriage for allowing her to feel safe enough to explore nonmonogamy with her husband. She explains, "that anchor and that safety allowed me to have that discussion to open it up."

We often think of marriage as a way to close yourself

off and become a world of two. But sometimes what it's really doing is giving you the support to explore the world more openly than ever before.

Look, I love to talk. I can spend a whole day endlessly chatting about anything from pop culture to my greatest trauma without a moment's hesitation. But all that swagger disappears the moment I have to openly talk about sex with my partner. This obviously poses a problem because being able to talk about sex with your partner is…pretty freaking important. As Michelle put it, "sexual communication is, to me, the foundation of having a healthy sex life… If you can't talk about sex, then how are you going to have really good quality, fulfilling sex? Based on your own definition, not mine."

So what do you do if you're like me and openly talking about this part of your relationship makes you want to hide under the covers (alone)? Thankfully, there are resources that can help get the conversation started. Michelle has a free download on her website called *The Sexual Communications Handbook* that includes over 200 sex-based questions. You don't need to have a specific topic or goal in mind to get comfortable talking about this stuff. Sometimes keeping it broad or tied to a fun game is a great way to get used to being more open. It's also helpful to deconstruct any harmful or misleading beliefs you already have about sex that might be making you squeamish or ashamed. As Michelle says, "exposing yourself to sex positive and accurate sexual health information" is a great way to start to reframe your understanding of humans as sexual beings. So don't feel shy about following an informed and progressive sex educator on Instagram or TikTok. It's not only good for your marriage, it's free!

Acquiring the tools to talk about sex with your spouse will also make it easier to navigate periods of major change. And yes, I am finally talking about the boogey monster of marital sex: children. Dr. Nikki tells her patients it's important to openly acknowledge that "kids change things: your relationship to your body, your relationship to understanding yourself and they definitely shift the dynamics and the relationship." But they don't have to kill your sex life. Michelle agrees: shifts happen, after all, but we can be more in control of the length and direction of that shift than we might think. She shares, "You might have to think a little more creatively around when you can have sex and what sex looks like now." She also asks couples if they can be okay with less than ideal sex for a period of time until there is space and energy to rebuild a more fulfilling sexual relationship as the kids get older. Because sometimes other things are going to take priority—like a screaming infant. And that's okay. Babies don't stay babies forever!

Now, this doesn't mean you should forget about sex until your kids move out. Instead, it's possible to establish some limits with our children early on. For example, teaching them that, unless it is an emergency, they don't get access to you at certain times. Dr. Nikki insists that it's "healthy for you to assert boundaries for yourself that gives you time to just recenter and reconnect and be with your partner and remind yourself why you chose to have babies with this person and build your life with this person." Obviously this approach is possible only with slightly older children, but knowing that you can one day implement it might reduce some of the worry that you'll never get a moment to yourself for at least 18 years. In the meantime, Michelle suggests maintaining an attitude of prioritizing your dyad. It can feel instinctual to always let the kids come first, even above your connection with your partner, but as Michelle points out, "this couple is what holds everything else together." So putting time and care into that relationship isn't forsaking your children's needs. It's really just a different and effective way of caring for the whole family unit.

Another situation when it's necessary to be skilled at communication is if one partner decides to transition or explore their gender identity. This can encompass a wide range of changes, from dressing differently to gender affirmation surgery. When someone transitions with hormones, Michelle says, it can have a big impact on the person's body and sex drive. It's useful to be able to address these potential differences directly instead of pretending they aren't happening. Maybe your partner wants to be touched in a new way, which would be impossible to know without talking about it.

Gender journeys often impact the person's partner in a

way that can be uncomfortable to discuss, too. A partner might be worried about coming off as unsupportive or offensive if they mention whatever their partner's transition means for them. But it is still important to actively make space for that conversation. The reality is that there can be a grief process, during which the nontransitioning partner is letting go of their previous conceptualization of the relationship. They might be adjusting to calling their spouse a new name or potentially interacting with their body in a different way than before. We have to make room for the nontransitioning person to reorient themselves.

If your partner transitions and you didn't see it coming, what will help carry you through the process, Dr. Nikki says, is having "genuine care about the other person's well-being. Like, I am committed to you as a human in your journey of being your best self, because you matter to me." Sometimes that means remaining married. Sometimes it means getting divorced but staying close friends. I'm not going to lie and say that *all* marriages will survive one partner transitioning. But I think it is far more likely than we may be led to believe, especially as we are starting to move away from rigid, binary thinking around sexuality. This is yet another area of marriage where the ability to roll with the unexpected can really pay off. Being flexible has never hurt when it comes to the bedroom, after all. (Imagine me winking at you right now.)

After all my (uncomfortable) conversations for this chapter, my biggest takeaway is that the worst thing for your sex life isn't children or monogamy. It's avoidance. Not attending to a disconnection or problem in the bedroom . can have ramifications throughout your entire relationship. As Michelle put it, unaddressed sexual issues can grow into a full-blown monster wreaking havoc on all areas of your connection. Taking a proactive approach by addressing issues right away or having preventive practices in place will ultimately save you a lot of time and effort. (In this instance, a preventive practice could be: *my partner always cooks dinner for the whole family on Thursdays and then we often have sex after because I'm not as tired.* That type of arrangement seems far more fun than other preventive measures like taking vitamins!)

When I asked Dr. Catalina if the whole idea of marriage was even realistic in today's society, she replied, "It all comes down to what [does the couple] think? That's all that matters. It doesn't matter what society thinks." So basically, if a married couple thinks marriage is realistic for them, it *becomes* realistic. They are the ones setting the terms and they know what they are capable of or want to be capable of. And *that* is the type of marriage they agree to. I think this method of constructing our own definition of something can also be expanded to our sex lives. You get to decide what a fulfilling sex life looks like for you as a couple. Not magazines or movies or your friend circle. You. And then, if you keep that agreement going—and make changes as needed—you're crushing it in the sex department.

With all that in mind, here are some questions to consider:

QUESTIONS TO ASK YOURSELF:

- Have I absorbed any harmful or inaccurate beliefs about sex? How do I plan to deconstruct them?
- When have I felt the most sexually fulfilled? What do I think helped lead to that outcome?
- Do I tend to have spontaneous or responsive desire? If I am more responsive, what is likely to turn me on?
- What are some non-penetrative sexual acts that I enjoy?
- Are there any barriers that tend to prevent me from feeling sexual? (For example, stress, poor body image or a bad sleep schedule.)

QUESTIONS TO ASK YOUR PARTNER:

- What would a fulfilling sex life look like for us?
- If we ever have an issue in our sexual relationship, what would be the best and least hurtful way for us to address it?
- Is there anything I might not already know about your body or sexual desire that you want to share?
- What do you think we should do if one person is in the mood and the other one isn't? How can we avoid anyone feeling rejected in those moments?
- What am I doing right in the bedroom? (So you can do more of it!)

Whew! Another tough topic down! Two more to go. You know what they say, marriage is a marathon, not a sprint. (I'm assuming someone has said that at some point!)

9
FOR WORSE AND
FOR POORER

When Things Go Wrong

In the 45 years that my parents have been married, they've been through a lot. My dad got diagnosed with multiple sclerosis in his early thirties. My mom had multiple knee surgeries with long recoveries and complications. Their older daughter (my sister) went through a rebellious teenage phase where she hated our family. Their younger daughter (me) became mentally ill with OCD as a preschooler. And a bunch of beloved family members died both expectedly and unexpectedly during that time. But when I asked them what was the most challenging hardship they've faced as a couple, they both agreed it was fighting over my childhood dog.

Having directly experienced this perilous period in our family history, I can confirm that it was indeed a rocky time. We had gotten Micki, an adorable wheaten terrier, when I was six to help with my contamination OCD through exposure therapy. But by the time I was 12, my father was sick of being tied down to a dog and having to occasionally clean poop off the rug. He wanted to give her away and my mom thought that was absolutely bananas. It might seem surprising that a fight over a dog led to the worst time in their marriage—especially when they have navigated so much before and after this point. But there was one key element that made this decision different from all the other tough moments. They wanted two different things.

You see, all that other awful stuff—the fear of not knowing what a life with MS would look like, the grief of losing parents and a sibling, parenting troubles—were things they could tackle as a team. The problem wasn't between the two of them so they could join forces against the outside issue. But when it came to the decision over Micki they were on opposite sides of the negotiating table and one person was going to end up pissed. I don't know what kind of conversations went on behind closed doors, but I do know my mother lost and/or conceded. Micki was rehomed to family friends who loved her as much as we (maybe minus my dad) did. Now, over twenty years later, Micki is still a sticky subject. When I asked my mom how they moved past it, her answer wasn't clear-cut. It seemed to be a mixture of time and holding on to a touch of resentment. But it didn't break them. They even got another dog years later who my dad grew surprisingly attached to.

As I talked to more and more married couples, a familiar theme emerged. Partners would either disagree over the hardest part of their marriage or their answer wouldn't be what you'd expect. It all goes to show that not only do we not know what hardships we will face in the future, we also aren't super great at predicting how we will react to them. No one goes into marriage expecting it to be easy breezy. Especially now that the problems we're facing as a society seem to always be snowballing, from the climate crisis to the spread of Covid. Most marriage vows even acknowledge the tough times to come because, at least for most millennials and Gen Z, it is hard to remember a time that *wasn't* tough (or terrifying in some way).

But is pledging to stay with someone "no matter what" realistic? Are all hardships actually survivable? Or are some experiences so traumatic that they fundamentally change the makeup of your relationship? And if that does happen, how do you know if you should cut your losses or try to adjust to your new reality together? To explore these anxiety-producing questions, I turned to two trauma-informed therapists, along with several couples who have made it to the other side of harrowing events. No one can predict what will happen to them, but maybe, with some insight and exposure to other people's experiences, we can all do a better job at preparing for whatever comes our way. (At least, that's what I keep telling myself.)

When I asked Melissa Moya, a licensed professional counselor, what are some of the most common hardships she's seen couples face, she didn't have to think for very long. Infidelity, unemployment, family planning issues, grief, mental health issues, substance use, and caregiving for an aging parent happen more often than we'd like. But there is another common problem that tends to fly under the radar despite its big impact. It has such a big impact, in fact, that when I asked Esther Boykin, a marriage and family therapist, the same question, it was her first answer: "periods of disconnection."

Yep. Out of all the possible difficulties a couple might face, Esther is most on alert for disconnection. While disconnection is far from a death sentence, it is somewhat of an inevitability. Esther explained that it is helpful to come to terms with "the fact that being in a relationship with another human being means that there will be periods of disconnection. You will hurt each other's feelings. You will disappoint… There will be periods of time when there is not even a thing to pinpoint."

When those times of disconnect naturally do happen, even if there is no clear reason or trigger, you don't have to panic to find a solution. You don't even necessarily have to retrace and figure out the cause. Instead, Esther says, sometimes all you need to do is have a conversation with each other that simply acknowledges what is going on so you can decide to "ride it out" together. What you don't want to do is ignore it because then the chasm can get bigger and bigger, making it harder to reach each other.

It's easy enough for me to accept that there will be periods of disconnection in my marriage. People get busy, life gets in the way and sometimes my mental health struggles make it difficult for me to be as present in my relationship as I would like. But after 35 years of being myself, I have a pretty good idea of how I handle tough periods. (Not too badly now that I'm medicated.) What I have much less evidence of is how John handles them or how we will handle them together. So I was curious if there are ways to foresee how you will handle hardship as a couple in the future.

According to Melissa, it's a half-yes. "You can't predict what you'll face, but I think that we can kind of see patterns in behavior... Even like the little things, how do they handle that? Are they somebody who shuts down and needs a lot of space to process?" It turns out that in some cases, examining how you or your partner handle the smaller frustrations in life can be a great indicator when it comes to how you two will handle the larger ones later.

Looking back, I realized that I was collecting this kind of information about John as we got to know each other without fully comprehending what I was doing. There was a night early on when we were trying to find a place to go to dinner before having to rush back to (virtually) watch a movie with friends. I think I gave some bad directions or didn't have a clear place in mind and felt myself tense in anticipation of him being annoyed with me because we had a ticking clock. Instead, he didn't seem to care at all. While other people I had dated would have been stressed out or frustrated, he was unfazed. I remember thinking, this seems like a good person to navigate life with. Little things don't throw him.

Another revealing moment happened after we moved in together and I had major knee surgery five days later. (I am my mother's daughter after all! Which means my knees, as we know from the beginning of this chapter, are garbage.) For weeks afterward, John had to be my caregiver—feeding me meals, taking me to appointments and helping me put my pants on. While I wouldn't wish MPFL reconstruction on my worst enemy, having the opportunity to see how John handled me at my most vulnerable was incredibly valuable and reassuring. He didn't get resentful or drop the ball. He didn't make my recovery about him or what he was missing out on. Instead, he behaved exactly how you would want a partner to act when you're in physical agony and occasionally vomiting from your pain medication. It might not have been a romantic time, but it was certainly an intimate one. And it made me feel more confident in my decision to hitch my horse to his wagon because I know how he "drives" (or whatever you do with a wagon to make this metaphor work).

To this point, Esther notes that "talking about going through hard times is not the same as going through hard times." Even though you might think you know how you or your partner are going to respond to something, it's much harder to put your money where your mouth is. So while it might seem advantageous to sit down and come up with a structured plan for how you will navigate specific issues if they come up, Esther thinks your time will be better spent developing the skills to 1) have difficult conversations, 2) stay emotionally connected, and 3) be vulnerable and emotionally safe with each other. Working on those muscles as a couple will serve you more in the long term than attempting to prepare for specific bad outcomes.

We're often told that good communication is the be-all and end-all superpower in relationships. But to Esther's point, direct communication can't do its job if couples aren't properly *emotionally attuned* to each other. We have to make each other feel emotionally safe while we express ourselves, instead of just focusing on the expressing. If emotional safety is missing, then it doesn't really matter how good we are at intellectualizing a problem. When the shit hits the fan, Esther asks, "do you turn toward each other in that moment or do you sort of turn inward or toward other people?" Being able to look at each other and say, "we're going through this thing together and it's really hard and really painful but...you're my person... and I'm your person" is powerful—even if no immediate shared solution presents itself for whatever is going on.

Unfortunately, many people struggle to access this kind of vulnerability in their marriages. It's a scary thing to expose all of your greatest insecurities, fears, and needs to another person—even if that person is your spouse. Pride, avoidance, and past trauma can all get in the way of that kind of communication. When a couple struggles to be this open, both partners, Esther says, can be "longing for some kind of emotional soothing and connection" but somehow fail to get it from each other. That's when a sense of loneliness and disconnection is likely to kick in. A couple can then end up drifting further and further apart even though what they really wanted was to reach for each other.

This is why so many therapists emphasize getting in the habit of sharing how you *feel* about certain events or interactions, and not just talking about logistics. Maybe your partner doesn't know that you are scared for them to take a new job, because you've only talked about what their new commute will mean for the morning routine, and not what this major life shift is bringing up for you. Or maybe you don't realize how stressful it is for your partner when your parents visit because they only discuss what activities you will do while they're in town, and not how your mother activates their anxiety. By establishing a default of turning toward each other during smaller conflicts and life moments to discuss how you feel, you will be better equipped to turn toward each other during larger hardships because you will be accustomed to meeting each other's needs and viewing each other as a safe space. Practice makes perfect as they say. (And if not perfect, then much improved!)

You want to make a point of meeting each other's needs

both to improve your daily life and protect your union. Because if someone isn't getting their needs met by their partner, they are more likely to turn to other people for support. This can mean a family member or close friend. For some, though, it can mean an extramarital affair. I don't believe that all cheating can be linked back to some type of dysfunction in the relationship, or that affairs should be blamed on the cheater's partner for not satisfying their spouse's needs. People cheat for all sorts of reasons, including plain old opportunity. When affairs happen, it doesn't automatically mean there is nothing left to save. Sometimes, depending on the circumstances, it can be a wake-up call that things need to change. But whether both partners want to make those changes after that type of betrayal is totally up to them.

When Piper met Nick in her early 20s, she didn't have any illusions about marriage. Her parents had gone through a horrible divorce when she was young, and her mother, to this day, has yet to recover from it. But that didn't stop Piper from marrying Nick within eight months of their first date. Even though Piper had only dated women before Nick and he was over 15 years older. Sure, it was risky, but if things didn't work out, she could just get divorced!

Piper and Nick spent the first decade of their marriage taking care of Nick's ailing father until he passed away. Their age difference never impacted how they interacted as a couple. Piper always felt like Nick's equal. But Nick's age meant that his parents were older, which led to Piper's twenties being taken up by caregiving for her in-laws and becoming a mom. She never got to have an extended young adulthood like Nick. She shared, "There wasn't a period of time when I was just building what I wanted for me." Instead, Piper was thrown into the pull of familial obligations from the moment she said, "I do." And while she doesn't regret it, she did lose sight of herself along the way.

Even after Nick's father passed and they moved to a new area (with their child and Nick's mom), Piper realized she was still letting Nick steer the ship a bit too much. Compromise is best in moderation, yet Piper was drowning in it. Growing up autistic, she had gotten into the habit of assuming she was in the wrong because she felt so different from everyone else. This led her to believe that if there was something she wasn't happy about, it was somehow her fault and her job to fix it. It's easy to see how this snowballed into Nick's preferences getting prioritized over hers. As expected, this dynamic began to weigh on her, and over time she became depressed and struggled with suicidal ideation. It was in this fragile emotional state that Piper went through Nick's phone and found messages that would change their relationship forever.

First, some brief background on Nick. Over the process of Nick becoming a new father, he began to realize he was an alcoholic. So he decided to stop drinking for the good of himself and his family. A few years later, he went to see a concert out of town and ran into some people from his past, including a woman he had a casual sexual history with. He ended up breaking his sobriety the night of the concert and hooked up with his old fling. Piper wasn't aware of any of this at the time, but she could sense something was off about the trip. She thought he might have fallen off the wagon, but didn't think for a second that he had cheated. After that night, he never saw that woman in person again. But he did continue a sexting and flirting relationship with her for the next seven years—until the day that Piper found the messages on his phone.

Piper immediately called her best friend, who had been cheated on before, for support. Following her friend's advice, Piper sat Nick down later that day and said, "This is your only chance to tell me everything." And to Nick's credit, he did. He explained that he had only physically cheated that one time and he had no intention of doing it again. He admitted he had kept up the texting relationship to serve his ego. He made it clear he regretted his actions and was willing to do anything to not lose his wife. And most importantly, according to Piper, he didn't get angry at Piper for looking through his phone or attempt to blame her for any of it. He took full accountability for his actions and cut off all contact with the other woman that very day.

While Piper certainly isn't nostalgic about that time in her marriage, she does think it was a crucial turning point for them. Instead of pulling away from each other, the threat to their union brought them closer than ever. Although Piper considered leaving Nick at other times during their marriage, the thought didn't even cross her mind following his infidelity. Instead, they found themselves clinging to each other—both emotionally and physically—once the truth was out. Piper said they were "frantic, desperate, scared rabbits" who were trying to express their fear of losing each other through sexual intimacy. She shared, "I would never say I'd want to go through that again, but I do think that it was necessary for us to hit that crisis point, realize that we could lose what we have and that we wanted what we had and that we were willing to work on it."

Finding out about Nick's infidelity also allowed Piper to examine her relationship in a new light. Before she felt she should always follow Nick's dreams and direction. But now that he had so royally messed up, the illusion that he was perfect while she was flawed was shattered. She suddenly realized she didn't have to sacrifice everything for him. She was allowed to take up space in their relationship, too.

Piper decided she needed to get more comfortable telling Nick when she was unhappy. Hiding her feelings wasn't going to protect her from a bad outcome, so she might as well share more with him. And when it came to her pattern of conceding, she started to ask herself, "Am I compromising things that are fundamental for myself?" If the answer was yes, she stopped automatically giving in and started fighting for what she wanted. This led to a major shift in how she was showing up in her relationship.

Piper grew up surrounded by chaos and instability. It made her crave a calm and stable adult life. Getting divorced, she realized, "would disrupt all that and it wouldn't even be worth whatever I'd gain on the other end of it." So even though they have hit rocky patches since Nick's infidelity, she's learned to check in with herself. Is separation what she actually wants long-term, or is it just how she's feeling in that moment? By not making drastic decisions, she allows herself time to come back to her stable self and remember that she wants to make things work.

Although they emerged stronger after the affair, getting through one major crisis together hasn't made their marriage indestructible. Piper knows they need to reenter couples therapy to help them navigate new stages in their marriage. And they still occasionally fall back into bad patterns. But going through what they went through has highlighted the importance of finding a balance between love and commitment to the marriage. Piper explained, "one of those two things is going to be what's keeping you in the relationship at any point… Sometimes I'm feeling 80% love and passion for this person… Just 20% commitment… And then sometimes I'm feeling much more like, okay, 90% is just my commitment to being married to this person right now and I'm not really feeling the love and passion." But as long as some sense of both love and commitment still coexist, she doesn't care if the percentages fluctuate from time to time. They've been through worse.

When it comes to hardship and marriage, I think there are two distinct types. The first is a hardship between the couple, like an affair. And the second is a hardship that comes from an outside source but has a major impact on one or both partners, like getting fired or the death of a loved one. The problem with the second kind of hardship is that people can react to it in totally different ways, and that difference, if we aren't careful, can lead to disconnection or even resentment. Having hugely different responses to the same event could even make someone wonder if they are with the wrong person. Like, why aren't you as thrown as I am by [insert terrible catastrophe]? Why aren't we the same level of upset? It can end up making one or both partners feel like they are navigating this huge thing alone—which kind of defeats one of the main purposes of marriage.

So *why* do we and our partners sometimes react so differently to the same thing? For starters, of course, people's external reactions don't always reflect the extent of their feelings. Many of us know this intellectually, but struggle to wrap our heads around this fact when we see it in action. There are some people who need to process trauma by talking about it. But for others, Melissa says, repetitively discussing what happened "is their worst nightmare and it becomes retraumatizing." In these cases, it's not that they aren't impacted, it's that they have a different way of dealing with their hurt. But if you don't know this, and you are someone who likes to outwardly process, it can seem like your spouse is shutting you out or is "over it." When in reality, constantly talking about what happened might impede their ability to heal. Not to sound like a broken record, but this is another example where accepting that different things work for different people will serve you and your relationship. We don't want to judge how our partner deals with pain or grief—as long as they are dealing with it in their own way.

Melissa also points out that your partner doesn't need to be your only support system during a difficult time. If you find that you want to keep talking about a situation, but your partner doesn't, maybe it's a great time to seek another resource, such as individual therapy, a support group or even verbal journaling. Finding other outlets doesn't mean you have failed to support each other during a difficult time. It means we are taking the sole pressure off our spouse to be our savior, and tailoring our support to what works best for us as individuals. (Personally, I often need a fun snack to find the will to keep going.)

Sometimes, though, a certain hardship really and truly won't impact both partners equally. For example, losing a parent might not feel the same as losing an in-law. But our partner doesn't need to feel our exact feelings to be able to care for us well. In those situations, it's natural, Esther says, for one person to shift into more of a caregiving role. We often think marriages should always be 50/50 but, Esther explains, "the reality is that sometimes one person's giving 100% and the other person's giving 10% because that's literally all they have, because they're struggling."

This type of dynamic doesn't work long-term, but it can definitely help get a couple through a period when one partner is more affected than the other.

At what point, though, is it unfair to keep up a 90/10 dynamic? And do we need to be mindful of how the suffering partner treats the caretaking partner during their tough time? Because, as Melissa notes, sometimes it's not just about the hardship itself, it's how the sufferer is responding. For example, if your partner loses their job, they might take it really personally. This could cause them to beat themselves up, or it might lead to them taking out their hurt on you. If that's the case and your partner is lashing out in response to something they are going through, Melissa suggests that you try to figure out "How long can I put up with this moodiness or this nastiness?" Once you've determined your boundary or timeline, then it's worth initiating a transparent conversation to let the struggling partner know you can see they are suffering and want to help. However, Melissa explains, if you're caring for them and empathizing with their struggle, and there's still an "unwillingness or maybe even an inability to work through it" on their end, it is not your duty to stay in a dynamic where your partner continues to treat you poorly.

In this kind of scenario, it's important to separate your feelings about your partner's hardship from your feelings about their *reaction* to it. Try to make it clear you are not upset that your partner is unemployed. You are upset because they are taking it out on you and being volatile or disrespectful. This isn't the same thing as leaving someone when they're down. It's an active decision to not tolerate mistreatment from your spouse. We all have a different threshold for how long we can stay in a situation where our partner is taking their pain out on us. The broader context of the situation also matters. But when both parties know that they can and should have a threshold of "enough is enough," that will hopefully alleviate any misguided guilt if one of you does decide to leave.

Sometimes when a horrible thing happens to us, it can change us fundamentally. That change might not result in mistreatment of our spouse, but it can lead to a level of dissociation from our previous self. It might feel like, "How can the person I am now, be in the same relationship as the old me when I am so different?" Navigating that type of disconnection is tricky, and sometimes it's hard to come back from. Melissa believes that in cases like these, "it's okay for people to give themselves permission to change, and to admit, I'm totally different because of this, and therefore I need something completely different."

I think these types of cases probably call for radical acceptance. Yes, if this thing *hadn't* happened then maybe your current marriage would still work, but the thing *did* happen, so you have to adjust accordingly. If you can fully accept that you are a different person now instead of trying to find your way back to who you once were, you can start to focus on where you want to go from here. Maybe you want to move forward alone. Or maybe you want to try to create a completely new relationship—even if it's with the same partner.

When Parker and Riley got married, they presented to mainstream society as a straight couple—even though they were both queer. But since their union, both Parker and Riley have come out as non-binary, and their parallel gender journeys came with one complication: how to have children. Parker had never planned to be a parent because their own parents had left a bad taste in their mouth. They simply didn't think of parenting as a positive thing in the world. But Riley had a different perspective, and expressed to Parker that they wanted to have kids. At first Parker rejected this idea, but over time, they changed their mind.

Parker and Riley became aligned on wanting to start a family, but they each had different ideas when it came to how to do it. Parker wanted to foster elementary-school-aged children and Riley wanted to try for a biological child. There is no real compromise between those two options, so Parker decided to give it a go biologically since it was so important to Riley. But despite agreeing to try, Parker didn't actually want to be pregnant. It felt incongruent with their body and gender identity. And attempting it the old-fashioned way also meant delaying Riley's medical transition because Riley couldn't go on hormones while trying to impregnate their partner. So when conception didn't happen naturally, Parker felt relieved. It was time to try to have a child a different way.

The couple quickly found that fostering or adopting presented a whole new host of problems. Even though it was Parker's idea to explore the foster system, they still had a lot of moral qualms with it. Parker had spent enough time researching to learn that many adoptees consider adoption to be trauma and interracial adoption often has tinges—if not large doses—of white saviorism. At the same time, they wondered if there was ever an ethical way to have a child since birth is inherently nonconsensual. Maybe, they thought, there is no "right" way to do it if a baby can't ask to be born in the first place. It was a moral dilemma without a clear answer, and Parker realized they might just have to live with the discomfort of being a part of a well-intentioned but problematic system.

So, at the beginning of the pandemic, Parker and Riley went through all the training to become foster parents. This forced some tough conversations and negotiations. Parker was interested in a wide range of ages, while Riley wanted to foster children under the age of four. Parker also initially had a desire to foster queer teens, but they learned through a brief experience that fostering teenagers wasn't the best fit for their family. Once they had narrowed down what they were both open to—children under four—they waited. Until one day they got a call. A nine-month-old baby, who had been in foster care since birth, was in need of a new placement. They learned that the baby, Emily, might become eligible for adoption. Riley and Parker instantly agreed to foster her.

As soon as Emily joined their family, Riley and Parker thought they would be able to move forward with officially adopting her. But in the summer they hit a roadblock, and suddenly they were in a cycle of uncertainty where adoption seemed impossible, then possible again, and so on. They had both grown to love a little girl whose future wasn't completely in their control. It was a complex problem to navigate because neither of them knew if Emily was going to be taken away or not. They didn't know how much time or energy to spend preparing for the worst.

Following that summer, Parker felt pressure to not get too attached to Emily in an effort to protect themselves, which is a tough sort of emotional gymnastics. Parker and Riley ultimately decided that "we can't spend too much time grieving something that may or may not happen... pre-grieving doesn't actually help." So they have tried to swap out worry for hope. They are both determined to stay in Emily's life even if they aren't able to adopt her. And instead of focusing on what might happen in the future, they try to focus on all the love and care they have already given Emily during such an important developmental time in her life.

Throughout all this, Parker and Riley had long discussions about whether or not they would foster again. It is not an easy conversation since Parker has found navigating the foster care system to be traumatizing—even as a person with a lot of privilege. So they are rather reluctant to do it all over. Plus, even if Emily's adoption goes through, it's not all sunshine and roses. Parker doesn't want the legal process to unfairly erase Emily's family of origin. But that might be another outcome they can't control, because it is currently unclear what role Emily's biological family wants to play in her life.

Nothing around parenthood has been clear-cut or easy for Parker and Riley. Yet, despite all this strain on their marriage and mental health, Riley and Parker remain strong partners. They have been each other's secure base through everything. And considering Parker is estranged from their family and Riley has a complicated relationship with their own, this support is crucial. Parker knows it might sound like they're codependent since they are "so much for each other." But the reality is that both Riley and Parker came from traumatic backgrounds and they have healed together. They are each other's main source of family. And even with the various hardships created by trying to *grow* that family, their marriage doesn't seem to be in danger of falling apart. Their love for each other is not tied to the outcome of their circumstances. It is entirely their own.

If it isn't obvious by now, love and commitment don't cause two people to fuse into one single entity. Instead, married life is often an (endless) series of compromises because you are two distinct people with two distinct points of view. So how do you navigate different desires without them tearing you apart? Especially if you are arguing over something more substantial than what movie to watch. Esther says that when a couple wants different things you have to ask, "Where's the bridge between what you need and what I need?" This type of exploration allows us to honor our differences and be flexible, while remaining direct about our boundaries. It's an approach that can help reveal a middle ground that might otherwise be overlooked.

Even so, difficulty and hardship often act like a pressure cooker in a marriage, and you don't always know if your relationship will survive or be recognizable once the dust has settled. It's helpful to remember that we don't have to fight to stay together at all costs in all conditions. A happy life is not measured by the length of your marriage, but its quality. As a couples therapist, Esther feels she needs to let people know, "It's okay to look at the landscape of your relationship and say, 'I don't want to do the work required for this to be a sustainable relationship where we both feel honored, respected, loved, and are able to thrive." Often, it's not a question of if a relationship can be saved, but if you have a strong enough *desire* to save it. Because bringing a relationship back from the brink isn't easy. It takes a lot of time and effort that some people would (understandably) rather spend elsewhere.

Esther herself has watched a lot more couples come to terms with the fact that fighting for their marriage isn't how they want to spend the next decade of their lives. They realize they can opt out of their current relationship and find partners who are better suited for them. Esther explains, "That doesn't mean that you didn't love each other, and it doesn't mean you didn't honor the commitment of marriage."

I love this framework. Instead of rejecting or regretting your shared history, you're simply accepting that you've changed. Some people are able to claw their way back to who they were before, or, instead, forge a new dynamic that works for them. And some people part ways. Despite what historical stigmas around divorce or breakups might lead you to believe, one option is not more moral or "right" than the others. All three are morally neutral if handled with care and mutual respect.

When it comes to the whole rigidity of "till death do us part," Melissa agreed that it's important to give yourself permission to change and to walk away. As a society, we can begin to allow ourselves the freedom to look at marriage as a continuous choice and not a life sentence. In the same way that we can't predict what hardships will come our way, we can't know for sure how we will handle them. We might feel like giving up at the first bump in the road. Or we might find a way to endure more than anyone would think possible.

Please read this next story with care. There is mention of rape.
When Cora met Jack seven years ago, she had never dated a man before and identified as a lesbian. So when she expressed interest in him after breaking up with her girlfriend, Jack was surprised. He was unemployed and

taking care of his ailing grandmother when they began dating, but Cora saw his decision to put his life on hold to care for his family as a testament to his good character. She felt that Jack was a "diamond in the rough," and nine days short of their one-year anniversary, they got married.

Their desire to build a family is where things got a bit tricky. They wanted to have a baby and were struggling to conceive, but doctors refused to take their fertility concerns seriously because they are both plus-size. As a reult of this anti-fat bias, they didn't get offered the same level of medical care other people receive. They were also going through all this while sharing a cramped small studio apartment, which exacerbated everything.

One night, Cora started to experience severe pain and excessive bleeding. She ended up needing surgery to remove a cyst. After the procedure, her doctor advised her to use an IUD for a month or two in order to regulate her lining and make it easier to get pregnant. Cora welcomed the break from trying to conceive since sex was always a tricky part of their relationship. While Cora loved Jack, she still found herself more sexually compatible with women, so sex wasn't a huge priority in their relationship. But in order to get pregnant, you have to have scheduled sex, which felt like a burden to both of them.

Adding to the strain of infertility, Jack had recently taken a job that put them on opposite schedules. They didn't really have time to get into the flow of being newly married because they were barely seeing each other. Instead of trying to work through it, they filed for divorce.

The problem was that neither one of them actually *wanted* to get divorced. They were playing a game of relationship chicken. It was basically a prolonged battle to see who would admit they wanted to stay married first, and neither one of them made any effort to move out or move forward with a legal separation. It was a strange, disconnected time in their marriage where, according to Cora, the normal rules didn't apply. So Cora decided to go on a date with a man she met on an app. It was a horrific experience. The man locked her clothes and personal belongings away, forcing her to stay the night, and raped her. She was only able to escape once his roommate appeared the next morning.

It took Cora a long time not to blame herself and begin to heal. As time went on following her assault, things started to get better in Cora and Jack's marriage. They became intimate with each other again, and even began to notice some telltale signs of pregnancy. She went to Walgreens to get a test. It was positive. Her pregnancy was then confirmed at the ER—despite her IUD and PCOS diagnosis. The doctor explained that the embryo had latched on to a side of her uterus far enough away from the IUD for it to take hold. Cora was filled with a rush of emotions at the surprising news. She knew she wanted the baby and her quick conception math also seemed to imply that Jack was the biological father. They were finally going to have a child.

In a perfect world, the story would end here. But in the real world, Cora had a hell of a time bringing her little girl into the world. She had a high-risk pregnancy and was diagnosed with both diabetes and preeclampsia. Her premature labor was over thirty hours long. But nothing prepared her for when Cora realized from her newborn's features that her rapist might be the father. The moment only lasted a second or two before Cora's maternal instinct took over, and all she cared about was making sure her preemie baby was going to be okay. Her daughter had to stay in the NICU for 43 days, and during that time, Cora shoved her daughter's unclear paternity to the back of her mind. She was too focused on keeping her baby alive. But then doctors brought up the possibility of a genetic condition that might help explain some of her daughter's health problems. They wanted to test to see if either of her parents were carriers, because if it was indeed a hereditary condition, the predicted outcome was much better than if it wasn't hereditary. If neither parent carried the gene, the child's life expectancy was only eight or nine years. Suddenly it was vitally important to know who was the biological father.

After Cora and Jack did a paternity test, their fears were confirmed. Jack wasn't the biological father. Despite this devastating news, they still wanted to do everything they could for their daughter. So they made the difficult decision to contact Cora's rapist and ask if he would do genetic testing. At first, her rapist agreed, and acknowledged and apologized to Cora for the assault. But not long after, he changed his tune. He not only refused to get the blood test, but he voiced a desire for joint custody of Cora and

Jack's daughter. And he was going to take them both to court to try to get it.

What happened next is maddening. Cora and Jack hired a guardian ad litem to review everything and make a suggestion to the court in the best interest of their daughter. The guardian ad litem advised the judge to not change the paternity on the birth certificate, which was currently listed as Jack. This made a lot of sense, because on top of being a known rapist, the man asking for paternity had also shared breeder fantasies with Cora that bore tinges of pedophilia. This was not the sort of person anyone would want in their child's life, and yet somehow, the judge awarded the rapist paternity. It's not standard practice to go against the guardian ad litem advice, and Cora and Jack were understandably horrified. They now had to enter a yearslong custody battle with a man who had already caused so much trauma in their lives.

When we think about what hardships we might face in a marriage, fighting with a rapist over custody of your child probably isn't the first thing that would come to mind. Some people might have left their marriage after an instance of trauma, assault, or finding out they weren't their daughter's biological father. But that's not what happened here. While they can't control what the courts will ultimately decide, Jack has spent the last four years showing up every single day as his daughter's dad.

Despite the custody battle hanging over them, Cora and Jack have continued to move forward as a family. They both wanted to have another child, and after a full year of infertility, Cora was finally prescribed medication that helped her conceive within a month. She had an easier pregnancy this time. While their son was also born premature, after 41 days in the NICU, he was developmentally caught up and ready to be discharged. Cora shared that once he was home, "it was just a healing experience of getting to like, enjoy my motherhood." Their family felt like it was officially complete.

Cora and Jack's experience with hardship is an extreme one and might not seem inherently relatable. But I think it reveals how much the same marriage can change with time and circumstance. I don't know if Cora and Jack will remain a couple forever, but what they went through certainly bound them together as parents and people. And that is something worth celebrating.

I didn't share these stories with you so you could brace yourselves for the exact same scenarios. Every couple goes through their own unique difficulties. But sometimes, by seeing what's been possible, we can become a bit more confident in our future selves. We can't know for sure how we will handle one hardship versus another. But we can try to create a foundation that isn't rocked so easily by outside stressors. And I know for me, seeing other people be able to do that makes me less scared about what's to come. (Even if I would prefer to just have one of the #blessed lives and never have to deal with anything more challenging than a delayed flight on our way to vacation.)

As I think about my marriage, I don't know what we will be able to sustain or endure. But I do know we will try to tackle whatever might come our way as a team. Because the two of us against the world feels a lot more manageable than facing everything on my own. It's kind of the whole reason I want to get married in the first place.

Now that we got through the hard part, here are some things to ponder:

QUESTIONS TO ASK YOURSELF:

- Do I spend too much time preparing for bad things that might not even happen? What am I mentally bracing myself for *right now*? Is there a better place for me to exert my mental energy?
- Can I release myself from the expectation that I should be able to predict the future and my reaction to it? Can I do the same for my partner?
- What strengths of mine will I be able to lean on if/when I face a major difficulty? How can I continue to nurture them?
- Am I harboring any views about myself that are getting in the way of having the type of relationship I want?

QUESTIONS TO ASK EACH OTHER:

- How do we want to handle periods of disconnection? Can we agree to not be defensive or jump to conclusions if/when we encounter them?
- Have you ever been through a negative experience that fundamentally changed you? If so, in what ways?

- Is there anything about the way I handle tough situations or everyday frustrations that worries you?

I can't believe it! We only have one chapter left in this book about marriage. Seems like a good time to talk about divorce!

10

AS LONG AS WE BOTH SHALL LIVE (OR TOLERATE)

Reframing Divorce

Despite everyone constantly shouting that *half of all marriages end in divorce*, that simply isn't true anymore. The divorce rate has actually been going down since the '80s, and *TIME* reported in 2018 that the statistic is much closer to 39%. Arielle Kuperberg, the sociology professor I spoke to in the first chapter, also pointed out an interesting trend: "baby boomers are the most divorced generation of any generation"—yet their millennial children haven't followed in their footsteps. So why do we still assume 50% of marriages are doomed?

This is likely because we haven't adapted to the new state of marriage where fewer people are getting married, and the people who do tend to be older and more financially secure. This new approach allows people to be more thoughtful about if and when they get married. But that doesn't mean divorce is no longer an issue. Thirty-nine percent of marriages ending in divorce is still rather high. And the rate of divorce goes up even more for second and third marriages. There are also some troubling gender-based trends that feel important to point out. According to the American Sociological Association, women initiate around 70% of divorces, which starts to make sense when you realize men get significantly more health benefits out of marriage than women. (Or if you've ever had to spend a lot of time with your dad's friends.) It seems we are still a ways away from truly egalitarian marriages or divorces being the norm. But at least we are starting to conceptualize divorce differently thanks to changing social customs and more open-minded generations.

It might seem strange to end a book about marriage by doing a deep dive into divorce, but I think it would be stranger not to. If you're weighing whether to sign up for marriage, wouldn't it be helpful to have insight into what might happen if things don't work out? Even upbeat medication commercials have voice-overs about potential side effects. We can't properly talk about marriage without bringing up the D word because, even if we avoid saying it out loud, it likely lives in the back of our minds. Or maybe in the front, if we're having a particularly frustrating day and our partner won't stop chewing so loudly. The fear of getting divorced can range from a light hum to an overwhelming cacophony in our anxious brains. It's the sort of worry that not only prevents people from getting married, it keeps people locked in bad marriages. But what are we really so afraid of?

For a long time, there weren't any nuanced conversations around divorce. Society simply deemed it a horrible moral transgression and a loud, glaring sign that a marriage had "failed." But much like modern marriage has adapted to the times, so has modern divorce (at least in some circles). And this changing tide of public opinion has allowed a window for us to approach marriage in a different way, too. If we no longer view divorce as a terrible fate that ruins lives and reputations, but as a natural part of some relationship cycles, getting married no longer comes with such high stakes. It's the difference between doing something really cool that might hurt you versus doing something really cool that might kill you. (Even if in this case, "kill" is a metaphor for destroying your entire life and social standing.)

I also think our changing relationship toward divorce has likely made marriage itself more generally appealing to certain people. Having an acceptable exit route can make it less terrifying to become a spouse—especially if you are a person who tends to feel trapped. Knowing that divorce is an option tends to alleviate a lot of commitment anxiety, even if it isn't very romantic.

There is an instinct to assume that the only successful

ALLISON RASKIN

marriages are the ones that last until death, and as soon as divorce enters the picture any good that came from your union evaporates. What I want to do is challenge that idea. I believe it's possible to still find the positive in a supportive and adaptive marriage, even if it's run its course.

I'm not here to promote divorce as a great option or a "get out of jail free" card. It can be extremely emotionally and financially draining to legally part ways with your spouse. And no one goes into a marriage hoping it will end this way. (Aside from some people looking to swindle a rich family and then skedaddle.) But divorce can be an opportunity for a fresh start if we let it. And understanding the actual process can take away some of our fears around it, which is why I interviewed both divorce lawyers and divorcees for their insights and expertise. There is a lot discussed in this chapter, but one thing that really stood out to me is that even after everything these people have witnessed or been through, almost all of them still see the appeal of marriage. Which is really saying something.

Renee Bauer is a divorce attorney, advocate and founder of the firm Happy Even After Family Law in Connecticut. She has also been divorced twice. This personal experience shapes the approach she takes with her clients and how she thinks about divorce in general. Renee is open about telling it straight: divorce sucks. But in her words, "you have to get through the muck of it before you can start to come out and heal." She encourages her clients to "allow yourself to feel the grief. Allow yourself to sit in the sadness."

Likewise, Nicole Sodoma, a self-described marriage-loving divorce attorney, believes that for many people, "divorce can feel a lot like death." You are experiencing a grief that comes from laying your marriage to rest and saying goodbye to the future you had planned and the life you have. You have to make space for that grief and step in to care for yourself. You can't bypass the hurt by trying to put a Band-Aid on your heart and rushing into the next stage of your life. But you should try to remember that the pain won't last forever.

One popular resource that newly divorced people often seek during the grieving period is a divorce support group. Finding community, especially during a life transition that might otherwise make you feel like an outsider, is hugely helpful. You just want to make sure, Renee cautions, that you choose a group that is focused on uplifting each other. You don't want to fall into a community that's focused on "complaining about everything that's wrong with your ex because that doesn't help you heal. That just keeps you stuck in the anger and resentment." And while anger and resentment can be a fun place to visit from time to time, it's not where you should set up shop if you want any real shot at moving on.

Another big part of the healing process, according to Renee, is being honest with yourself about "what you contributed to in the breakdown of your marriage." Aside from abusive relationships, both parties are often responsible for what happened in *some* way, even though we obviously don't want to admit that. Figuring out what you did wrong can also help you form better relationships in the future because you aren't as likely to repeat the same patterns or continue to pick people who aren't the right match for you. Divorce offers an opportunity for a new level of self-awareness that you might otherwise have been avoiding. It is a shame not to take it—even if doing so means you might feel like the "bad guy."

That said, it's important to not solely focus on the negative or your past mistakes. To counterbalance the loss that inevitably comes with divorce, Renee encourages people to actively add new things to their life. Is there something you've always wanted to try but never had time for before? Maybe your partner hated to travel but now you can finally see the set of *Mamma Mia!* (Greece) in person. Maybe you could never join a book club before but now you can because your ex is with the kids on Thursdays. Maybe you finally have a moment to take a freakin' bubble bath. Renee also believes it is vital during the healing process to "start to figure out who you are again and to start to take care of yourself." Even if the idea of treating yourself to a nice solo dinner feels foreign and perhaps a little bit sad at first. (We need to reclaim the power of a solo dinner. Everything you want to eat without any of the small talk? Sign me up!)

Everyone has a different relationship to marriage while they're in it. For couples who have been living separate lives, getting a divorce might not change all that much.

But for people whose identities are largely tied up in their marriage, it can feel incredibly disorienting to suddenly find yourself unmoored and single. Nicole put it perfectly: "The hard truth of the dissolution of a marriage is that, while it takes two to say 'I Do,' it takes only one to say 'I Don't.' Whether you're the one who wants out or the one that didn't see it coming, how you receive it, how you respond to it, is still a choice you *do* get to make."

We can't force someone to stay married to us, nor should we want to, but we can choose how we want to move forward. We can long for the married person we once were, or we can find a way to redefine ourselves outside of partnership. Heck, we can even throw a divorce party to celebrate our new start. This would have been unheard-of a few decades ago but is now a surprisingly festive trend. (I'm personally quite tickled by some of the signage including, *I Do, I Did, I'm Done!*)

When Laura Stassi, the creator and host of the popular podcast *Dating While Gray*, married her now ex-husband in 1983, she never imagined herself divorced. Mainly because she "grew up in a traditional-values family where divorce happened only if there was an 'outrageous' issue, like alcoholism or abuse." This mindset meant she grew up judging people who got divorced. In fact, despite hosting an entire show about the potential of life after divorce, she still finds herself being "a little judgy" or catching herself wondering what's preventing people from being able to make it work. So it probably isn't surprising that she herself tried very hard to salvage her almost 30-year marriage, despite the fact that their relationship was, to put it politely, less than ideal.

When I asked Laura why she wanted to stay married so badly, she replied, "I really think I had low self-esteem." There were other factors too. She hadn't been working and was worried she wouldn't be able to financially support herself. She felt familial pressure to stay married. She didn't want to crush her two children. And, quite simply, she liked being married. She liked being part of a couple. At the time, she hadn't realized there was another factor influencing her desire to stay: she didn't want to be another divorce statistic. Social norms and standards might've been changing, but Laura still felt constrained by the traditional marriage setup she'd been sold since childhood. You know, the one where two people just stick it out no matter what to avoid public disgrace.

I'll admit that the story of Laura's marriage can feel a bit like a cautionary tale against the whole institution. Here is this smart, funny, loving woman whose inner light was diminished for decades because she was too afraid to face the ramifications of ending her marriage. They had married so young and she wasn't properly prepared for all the ways two people could grow apart. To further complicate matters, her husband "developed companionship and solace with other women," but refused to actually leave his marriage. Laura often jokes, "he didn't want to get divorced, but that doesn't mean he wanted to be my husband." What she saw as his passivity combined with

Laurie's insistence on trying to make it work led to several iterations of their relationship before she finally cut the cord for good.

The exact details of how Laura's marriage came to a slow end are a bit murky since she doesn't want to share too much for the sake of her grown children. The short version is that when her kids were young, she discovered her ex "was in the throes of a sexual and emotional affair with another woman. He was apologetic and vowed to end it," so they stayed together "without ever working on their issues." They later spent nine months apart in 2010 after Laura "discovered another infidelity," before separating for good into two residences in 2013. Laura returned to her maiden name in 2014 in an effort to reclaim her own identity, but waited until 2015 to file all the paperwork to make the divorce official. From her perspective, her ex didn't seem to care if they ever got legally divorced so long as he could keep living his own life, but she knew she needed closure.

Once Laura was officially single, the world began to open back up for her. Laura didn't start to think of herself as attractive or a sexual being until after her marriage ended. For decades, she had felt like a mom. She had felt like a wife. But she had not felt like a woman. Hearing this was heartbreaking, but falling into this mindset wasn't Laura's fault. Growing up, Laura had "few role models of older single women happy and content on their own." She's become hopeful that unlike her generation "younger couples now recognize the importance of really maintaining your individuality." Because, married or not, it's essential to learn how to be happy on your own. Especially since many people end up outliving a spouse or find themselves unexpectedly single at some point in their lives.

Now in her sixties, Laura views marriage and long-term relationships differently than before. She is no longer willing to sacrifice herself in order to fit into someone else's life. She still believes that "marriage can be a beautiful thing," but she knows "there's no such thing as happily-ever-after as an end point." You have to continuously do the work to keep your connection alive and make your marriage a priority. And in her mind, her ex-husband didn't do that. Considering that she used to be someone who wanted to stay married at all costs, it's telling that she has gotten to a place where she doesn't think "there's any glory in sticking it out." She does believe, though, that once you are married or in a committed partnership you should "try to do everything you can to make it a good and healthy relationship for both people" instead of throwing in the towel as soon as the going gets tough. This is a much more nuanced take than what she grew up with: divorce is always bad and marriage is absolutely necessary and the premium state of life.

Laura hasn't had much luck finding a new long-term partner since her divorce. (Dating is complicated at any age! Just listen to her podcast!) But she has figured out how to feel whole on her own. She often tells recent divorcees, "There will come a day you're going to feel good.

Not you're going to feel better, but you're going to actually feel good again. And I think that's really important to remember." Laura has no plans to get remarried because she's done having children and it's financially complicated to join assets at her age. But she does hope to find a committed partner someday. And in the meantime, she's quite busy feeling good on her own, now that she can see how truly wonderful she is.

While the nitty-gritty of divorce proceedings differ significantly state to state (and country to country), I don't want to ignore some of the more common repercussions for divorcees. Getting divorced can have a negative effect on one's health and lead to a dramatic reduction in your standard of living, including where you can afford to live and your access to health insurance. It is also incredibly expensive to get divorced in the first place. When I interviewed Sandy K. Roxas, a family law and divorce attorney in California, she explained that as of 2022, a typical divorce costs anywhere from $5,000 to $10,000. But if a case is highly litigated, that number increases from "$50,000 to $70,000 before trial," she says. "If the case is litigated, at trial the cost can be $100,000. This is the cost for average parties who have children, a house, and some retirement savings." You don't have to be super rich (or super famous) to have a super pricey divorce. That's why Sandy is also a huge proponent of prenups because it "makes the divorce so much cleaner and easier and amicable."

When couples don't have prenups or postnups in place,

things can turn ugly rather quickly. There can be an instinct to want to provide *proof* that one partner was at fault—either because you think it will help get you a better outcome or simply because you want to feel heard. But attempting to do so, especially in states with no-fault divorce, can just end up wasting a lot of time and money. Sandy has had to repeatedly tell clients that "there's certain information that holds no probative value" so there is no point in trying to air certain dirty laundry in court. She understands the instinct to want to expose the full story and prove your victimhood, but it doesn't always serve the client to do so.

Renee shared that "a lot of times people advocate from a place of emotion rather than reason, and that's when you start to see increased attorney's fees and a prolonged process." She advises people to take a practical approach to their decisions instead of an emotional one. For example, many people try to fight to keep the family home even though it's not a smart financial decision. Turning to a financial adviser for their objective input is one way to prevent yourself from making less sensible, more emotional requests in the settlement.

Nicole also goes out of her way to let clients know it's not necessary to constantly be in touch with their legal team. She explains, "I'll tell my clients, don't email and text me or call me every single day. It's going to cost you a fortune. Let's be more efficient. Let's talk every Tuesday at 12:00 p.m." She also advises people to give themselves "a day off every now and again" from the whole process to recalibrate and breathe. You don't need to be in fight mode every single moment to properly protect yourself.

That said, divorce can bring out the worst in people. Sometimes you need certain safety precautions in place before moving forward with the process. Back in 2016, Sandy had an older client who had been married for 30 years but wanted out. Sandy, who is very attuned to the prevalence of interpartner violence in marriages, asked if her client's husband had any history of violence. Her client noted that he had raised his voice and thrown things, but had never been physical with her. Sandy then asked her client if she thought it would be safe for her to stay in the shared home during the divorce process. Her client said she wasn't worried, so Sandy believed her. Her client filed the papers and her husband was served on a Friday.

That Saturday, her client's children were worried because they hadn't heard from either parent. They had the police do a welfare check on the house. They discovered Sandy's client shot dead with the divorce papers on her lap. Sandy had to testify in the trial a year later and her client's husband was convicted of murder. She was left wondering if it was all her fault. But she realized—with time and therapy—that she wasn't to blame. She had asked all the right questions and people can be unpredictable. But the horrific murder has definitely stayed with her. She shared, "whenever clients come to me and they tell me there's any inclination of domestic violence, I immediately tell them, you need to leave the house."

I was hesitant to share this story at first because I didn't want to feed into fears about the repercussions of getting divorced. But it felt insincere to omit the darker sides of how partners can possibly react. It's an important reminder that people often need to go to different lengths to protect themselves based on the temperament of their (ex) spouse. And it is always better to be overly cautious when your safety is involved.

Despite everything she's seen, Sandy still believes "divorce gives a person a new beginning" and she's "never had a client say that they regretted getting a divorce." This is another through line I noticed during my investigation: not one person I spoke to regretted ending their marriage once the dust had settled. Even if there were vastly different amounts of dust.

Ezra hadn't identified as polyamorous when he first started dating Keith, the man who would later become his (legal) husband. He assumed he was too jealous for that sort of lifestyle. So even though Keith had never been in a monogamous relationship before Ezra, they decided to keep their relationship closed. But after a few years together, Ezra started to feel guilty that Keith was making such a huge sacrifice for him, so he agreed to try polyamory.

For the first year, they casually dated other people while also looking to add a third, more permanent, person to their relationship. That person ended up being a guy named Tim. Tim had a similar trajectory to Ezra. He was fine being part of a throuple but didn't want to be open with other people only to then feel guilty and change his mind later on. During this stage in their relationship, Ezra and Keith decided to get married for logistical reasons, including health care, finances, and the type of rights that were available only to spouses, not partners, in their state. Tim, who they both continued to view as an equal partner, was even the witness on their marriage document. The three men would have preferred to share marital rights among all of them, but the law is not set up for that. So they compromised, and only Ezra and Keith were legally bound to each other.

Flash-forward a bit. Tim agrees to add a fourth person, Lyle, to their relationship. This dramatically shifts the dynamics. When it was just the three of them. Ezra, Keith, and Tim were able to share a California king-size bed. But the addition of Lyle meant the poly quad★ had to split into two bedrooms. (★A poly quad is a polyamorous relationship between four people.) Ezra and Tim slept in one bedroom while Keith and Lyle slept in the other. But in his heart, Ezra was equally committed to all three of his partners. He even referred to Tim and Lyle as his husbands, despite being legally married only to Keith. At least when it came to his friends. Only about half of his family knew Ezra was poly and had three partners. But they all knew he was married to Keith and had welcomed him in with open arms.

Even though being poly had started as a way to appease his partner, over time Ezra came to love the benefits of the lifestyle. He shared, "One of the biggest advantages to having been in a multiple-person relationship is that you're not alone at any point. Because if one of your partners is going through something, you have someone else there to go, 'I'm also here with you trying to help them.' You're not the only person trying to be a shoulder to cry on." He also enjoyed the communal aspects of living together. When there are multiple people tackling all the chores, it doesn't break down into a dynamic where either "you have to do it or I have to do it" because there are other people there to help. Ezra thought he had stumbled into a wonderful setup—even if the law wouldn't properly recognize the commitment of their poly-quad relationship.

Then things imploded. Ezra had been with Keith for over a decade when he found his husband breaking the rules of their relationship by having unprotected sex with someone outside of their poly quad. It soon became apparent that Keith had been cheating on Ezra their entire relationship—both when they were monogamous and when they were open. Despite the betrayal, all three of Keith's partners were willing to try to stay and work it out. But they had one condition. They wanted Keith to get professional help with his mental health. Instead, Keith made it clear that he had no intention of changing his behavior or taking responsibility, and his situation escalated into a suicide attempt and psychiatric hold.

Ezra decided it was time to leave the relationship. And only Tim, not Lyle, was willing to come with him.

To say it is disorienting to realize that such a huge chunk of your life was built on lies is an understatement.

But as Ezra started to examine his marriage with the benefit of hindsight, he realized things had been deteriorating for a while. The poly quad had even gone to couples therapy before the blowup, but they never directly tackled their bigger issues. So instead of feeling like therapy had helped, Ezra was left with an unnameable negativity coursing through his relationships that made him mentally exhausted and confused. He found himself depressed and self-harming for the first time in his life. Ezra could sense things were off but he didn't know what was really going on with any of his partners. It was only after catching Keith cheating that he also learned Tim had been struggling with jealousy and Lyle had been feeling guilty about his inability to connect with Tim.

Once all of this came to light in the fallout of Keith's betrayal, Ezra felt clarity for the first time in a long time. He knew he needed to break away from Keith and start over. But Lyle wanted to stay with Keith, so Ezra and Tim were left to figure out what a life looked like with just the two of them. Ezra found himself grieving the end of his marriage while still in a relationship with Tim, his partner of nine years. Having this support was a blessing. Ezra shared, "I feel very lucky that I actually didn't have to come out of this alone... I can't imagine trying to handle this pain and anger and betrayal that has come about by myself."

For so many people, divorce can be incredibly isolating because no one else knows exactly what you're going through or what you lost. But by opening his heart to multiple partners in the first place, Ezra had a third witness to the breakdown of his marriage. Having another person validate his memories and experience ultimately helped his grieving process. He didn't have to wonder, "did that really happen?!" for very long, because there was another person there to say, "yes, it did."

At one point, Ezra wanted to marry all three of his partners. But now that he is divorcing Keith, Ezra isn't ready to jump into another marriage with Tim. He's seen how brutal the divorce process can be, and he's thankful he never merged bank accounts with Keith because it makes it slightly less messy. He and Tim still have a lot to figure out in terms of what they both want for the future as they process the trauma of their relationship with Keith. But that doesn't mean another marriage is completely off the table. Despite his divorce and preference for polyamory, Ezra continues to feel there is symbolic meaning to marriage. He explained, marriage "is concrete recognition of the fact that I have made a commitment to you. That I am going to be here, that I can't just pack up and leave the next day and have it be easy… I am willing to do this thing with you. I am willing to commit to you in this way." The commitment that comes with marriage is meaningful to Ezra—even if his first husband never took it seriously.

During our conversation, Nicole, who recently went through her own divorce, remarked, "I can't believe with the number of divorces that happen, we still get shamed." It is kind of shocking that this life event that happens to so many people continues to carry social judgment. According to the U.S. Census Bureau, there were 827,261 divorces reported in 2019. Which means over 1.6 million people in the U.S. alone went through the process in a single calendar year. And that was *before* everyone was forced to spend all day inside with only each other during the pandemic.

Yet, despite the frequency of divorce, it can be hard not to blame yourself. Nicole believes it's easy to fall into a mental spiral about what the end of your marriage signifies and how its "failure" reflects on you. That's why it's been important to her to actively change her mindset. She now views her decision to leave her marriage as a brave choice—not a shameful one. This shift was likely made easier given her environment. Nicole, by trade, is surrounded on a day-to-day basis by other people getting divorced. It's not as hard to foster an atmosphere of acceptance in this kind of setting as it is in others. There are still pockets and cultures that continue to have rigid, negative views about divorce despite the year on the calendar. And if you are a part of this type of environment, the social stakes of getting a divorce can seem too high to even contemplate.

Zainab, a first-generation Pakistani American, always knew she'd have an arranged marriage one day. But she didn't expect it to be sprung on her three days before her high school graduation. Yet that's when she found her mother waiting for her at the dinner table ready to pitch a man in his mid-20s who she thought would be an excellent match. Caught off guard, 18-year-old Zainab agreed to meet him. So the potential pair went on a group trip to an amusement park with both of their siblings. When she came home and her mom asked how it had gone, Zainab replied, "I don't know. I never talked to him." Later she heard her father tell someone on the phone that she was engaged, which was news to her. Apparently, her mother had taken her lack of an outright rejection to be an approval. She was now engaged to someone she didn't know at all.

And things didn't get better as they got to know each other. They got worse. Zainab quickly realized she was not compatible with this man in any way, but her parents weren't willing to listen to her objections. In their minds, her future husband checked all the boxes for an ideal son-in-law. He was smart, financially stable and from a good family. His personality wasn't a concern to them because marriage was all about adjustment. They allowed Zainab to have a long, three-year engagement until she finished college, but they wouldn't let her back out of the agreement.

So within a few months of graduating, Zainab found herself married and in a different part of the country with her new husband. All her worst fears were quickly coming true. Despite their previous conversations, her husband suddenly expected her to prioritize her wifely duties over continuing her education. He put pressure on her to start a family right away, which was a total reversal from what he had assured her while they were engaged. On top of his controlling behavior, he was also struggling mentally. Zainab is now a mental health professional, but at the time she wasn't knowledgeable about psychology. So she didn't realize her new husband had severe depression. It didn't help that when she mentioned his concerning behavior to his family, they brushed it off, because they didn't acknowledge depression as a "real" illness.

Things were so bad that when Zainab visited her parents that December, she ended up staying. She kept in touch with her husband over the phone for a few months, but their fights were constant and they disagreed on everything. By the time Zainab finally proposed getting a divorce, he instantly agreed. His only condition was to move forward in a positive way and never bad-mouth each other. She was happy to oblige. After all, he was a good guy—just not the guy for her. In the end, they were engaged for three years and married for six months.

Despite her unhappiness, Zainab took a huge risk by asking for a divorce. In her Muslim, Pakistani culture, women who get divorced are often viewed as tainted. There was a good chance Zainab would never be able to get married again because of her history. But in her mind, she realized "I'd rather be alone for the rest of my life than be with him." Except her decision didn't just affect her. Because Zainab is the oldest of 35 cousins, some of her family worried she was going to set a bad precedent for the family. One aunt cautioned, "If she's thinking of getting a divorce or gets a divorce, what's going to stop my daughter from getting one?" Luckily, another aunt stood up for Zainab and said it wasn't fair to put that kind of pressure on her. She wasn't responsible for the future decisions of her much younger cousins. She only had one life to live, and she needed to do what was best for her. She had to leave her marriage.

Zainab doesn't think she would have had the strength to leave without the support of her family. By the end of the short-lived marriage, even her mother was supportive of her decision. (Her father, on the other hand, not so much.) While Zainab felt relief about her mother's change of heart, she also held on to some resentment toward her mother for having forced her to get married in the first place. Why did it take so long for her mother to listen to her? She had protested the arrangement for years! The fallout of a marriage that could have been avoidable was all-consuming. Zainab found it hard not to cry all the time. She was only in her early twenties, but she didn't know how she could possibly move forward and build a new life for herself as a divorcee. So she stopped focusing on her romantic future. She turned to her career and her friends. Two things she hadn't been able to focus on while married. And as time went by and things started to feel normal again, she slowly found herself open to the idea of another arranged marriage.

This time though, things were going to be different.

Her parents weren't going to make the final decision, and Zainab would have a voice throughout the process. She would be presented with different options and then get to decide who felt right to her. This was all well and good, except for one slight detail. If this marriage didn't work out, she couldn't blame her family and would have to take responsibility. But the risk seemed worth it. She started to have conversations with her parents about what she was looking for in a husband. She wanted someone stable, but she also wanted someone she actually enjoyed spending time with—something that was sorely missing in her first marriage.

As her parents set out to find someone suitable, Zainab also took the search into her own hands by joining a Muslim dating app. But then her mom showed her a biodata, which is basically a résumé for dating, that was intriguing. She wanted to talk to her potential match, Malik, on the phone before meeting in person to suss him out, but his family didn't approve. So she went on another group date. Again, the group dynamic meant she didn't get to talk to him much, but her aunt's family was there and sensed he could be a good match. So Zainab got to know him and learned Malik actually had a lot of overlap with Zainab's first husband. He had been raised in Pakistan but moved to the U.S. a few years before. He was also an engineer. And he was divorced. But despite the similarities with her ex, their connection was completely different. She knew within a few months that she actually wanted to marry him. He felt the same way.

Now, Zainab is not only a wife but a new mom. Malik and Zainab both went through unhappy marriages before finding each other, but Zainab credits the success of their current relationship to their ability to be open with each other. Because, despite their chemistry, they've had a few differences to work through. Although they are both Pakistani, Malik was born and raised in Pakistan. He has a different outlook on the world than Zainab, who was born in America. For instance, he still thinks women are judged for being divorced so he doesn't want Zainab to be so open about her past. That same concern doesn't extend to his own divorce, though, because he's a man, and men aren't judged for the same things in his culture. But Zainab doesn't want to have to hide her history so they've had a lot of difficult conversations. Unlike in her first marriage, though, these conversations actually lead to compromise.

Getting through one divorce and making it out alive—and happily married—hasn't completely alleviated Zainab's fears around the process. If anything, she finds herself more worried about the social ramifications of a second divorce. Would a second separation make her untouchable? She knows if that were to happen she would ask herself questions like, "What is wrong with me? Why am I not able to stay with somebody?" But a newly awakened part of her is starting to recognize that relationships are about two people, and if they don't work out it's not that something is necessarily wrong with either party. There is something wrong with the connection.

I've often wondered about the appeal of getting married for a second, third or, if you are romance novelist Danielle Steel, fifth time. (I should note that after her last divorce, she has remained unmarried, and highly successful, for decades.) Is the harrowing process of getting divorced a deterrent to trying again, or does the desire to be married grow even stronger, overpowering the negative experiences?

Obviously, the answer is different for everyone. But research from Bowling Green State University shows that the overall rate of remarriages has gone down in recent years. One statistic that remains consistent, though, is that men are more likely to get remarried than women. Likely due to all those additional benefits they seem to get from it. Including having someone around to monitor their health and encourage them to actually go to the doctor.

I'll admit that while I'm totally understanding of people who get married twice, I used to be curious about the decision to get married for a third (or fourth) time. This curiosity wasn't about multiple serious relationships not working out. (Been there! Done that!) It's more about the decision to keep getting married instead of just cohabiting. Why bother going through all that legal turmoil again and again?

But then my conversation with Renee changed my perspective. You see, Renee, in addition to being a divorce attorney and advocate, is on her third marriage. I found this surprising because if anyone knows the impact of going through a divorce, it's Renee. Why would she take such a big risk for the third time?

When I asked her about it, Renee explained that her decision had less to do with the relationship between her and her now husband and more to do with their kids. She has one son from a previous marriage and her husband has three kids. She shared, "we wanted to show our kids the commitment that we had to each other and to being a family." She didn't want her son to have to tell people he lived with his mom and her boyfriend. I think Renee's reasoning here acknowledges that the designation of married, over cohabitating, still holds a different status in society. It evokes, correctly or not, a certain level of stability, especially when children are involved. If their kids had been older when they met, Renee isn't sure they would have felt the same desire to be a legally defined family.

For Renee, her issues were never with the institution of marriage so much as her choice of partners. She liked being married. But she met her first husband when she was still in college and they ultimately grew apart. And her second marriage was a bit of a rash decision that ended quickly. Despite this history, Renee explained, "I had this faith that the relationship in my head that I wanted was out there." She hadn't found it with her first two husbands, but she knew that it still existed. Then she met her current husband and he had all the pieces she'd been looking for. So after a few years of dating, she took the leap and got married again—despite what she referred to as the "fear factor." It might be her third marriage, but it's

her first time finding the right dynamic. It's another reminder that no two marriages are the same. But if you've
only been married once, you might not have a frame of
reference for what other types of marriages are possible.

Paul didn't cheat on his wife of over 20 years because he
is some evil mastermind or a heartless villain. He cheated
on his wife because he was raised to believe divorce wasn't
an option. That, plus a strong proclivity for avoidance. On
the surface, the broad strokes of Paul's divorce have all the
makings of a tabloid story. An older, successful man leaves
his family for a much younger woman after a steamy and
secretive affair. But once you learn the details, it feels more
like a train wreck that could have been avoided.

Growing up, Paul's parents behaved more like room-
mates than soulmates. Their priority was their children—
not each other. So when he started thinking about his
own life's trajectory, his main goal was to have children.
Marriage was more of an afterthought or a means to an
end. The woman he decided to marry was pretty, nice,
and easy to get along with. She seemed like a good person to start a family with. Sure, there was no passion.
There was no sense that she was the person he was meant
to be with. But he'd been taught to believe that "marriage is just an agreement" that you follow for the rest of
your life. He had been raised to be a good Christian man
and father. In his particular case, he had not been raised
to self-reflect or even stop to consider what kind of marriage he actually wanted.

For a long time, this approach to life worked for him. He had his two kids. He had his career. But then the pandemic hit and suddenly he couldn't ignore the extent of his unhappiness.

The monotony of his daily routine began to wear on him. He would wake up, go to work in his windowless basement, cook dinner, watch some TV and go to bed. He started to wonder, "Is this the way I'm supposed to be?" Was life just about killing time? Suddenly, he was forced to confront existential dread and misery head-on.

So he told his wife he wasn't happy. They decided to go to couples therapy, but couples therapy only works when people are willing to get vulnerable. And Paul wasn't used to doing that. He was used to pretending everything was fine and going through the motions. So that's what he would do in sessions. Looking back, he realizes he wasn't actually interested in making things better in his marriage. He just wanted to smooth things over. This prevented his wife from ever having the opportunity to form the type of connection he was looking for—which led him to find it with someone else.

Paul didn't set out to have an affair. He didn't even have a history of cheating. But when he started chatting with an attractive 30-something outside his usual coffee place, he made the snap decision to pursue her. And in order to have a shot with Lacy, he didn't mention he was married. After two weeks of dating, though, he finally confessed. At first, Lacy was furious and cut off contact. But after about a week, they were talking again. Their relationship only grew from there.

Despite his initial lie to Lacy and his ability to keep his affair from his wife, Paul doesn't think of himself as an inherently dishonest person. Instead, he views himself as a necessary protector, and one who often hides his own feelings for other people's benefits. This habit, though, set the groundwork for him to live a secret life instead of just asking for a divorce. So much pain and fallout could have been avoided if he had just been honest with his wife once he realized the extent of his unhappiness before even meeting Lacy. Instead, he schemed and strategized and, you guessed it, avoided.

As things got more serious with Lacy, Paul knew he would have to end his marriage. But then he got a job offer in a different state and a thought occurred to him. He knew his wife and children wouldn't want to relocate, so if he took the job, he would be able to move there on his own and frame it as shifting into a commuter marriage. He figured he could secretly take Lacy with him, set up a new life together, and then, from a safe distance, tell his wife the truth. Except, before he could execute his morally questionable plan, Lacy's mother interfered.

When Lacy's mom found out that her daughter was moving away with a mysterious boyfriend, she decided to do some digging. Lacy's mom quickly found Paul on Facebook, saw that he was still married and messaged his wife to tell her what was going on. At first Paul was furious, but now he appreciates being forced to come clean.

He could no longer avoid the truth in an effort to not be the guy who hurt his wife and kids. That version of himself, the good Christian father who never messed up, no longer existed. Instead, everyone, including Paul, was left to deal with the real version of him, for better or worse.

After finding out about Lacy, Paul's wife was the first one to mention divorce. But she quickly backtracked. She asked Paul if he would be willing to work on things and try to save their marriage. Paul told her no. Now that the cat was out of the bag, he found himself able to vocalize what he wanted for the first time. Even though it meant hurting someone who didn't deserve to get hurt.

Paul's relationship with his now ex-wife has always been complicated. It's clear that he has nothing bad to say and still cares about her. It's also clear that he never really gave their marriage a fair shot. Being with Lacy was the first time Paul ever felt properly in love because he actually opened up to her and allowed himself to feel seen and heard. He never gave his wife the same access. And realizing this was the most painful part for his wife because she had always wanted more from Paul. She told him, "I would have understood... You just never gave me that chance." Paul knows she's right. But, for whatever reason, he had gone so long without being open with her that it felt impossible to get there. With Lacy though, a person who had no expectations or preconceived notions about him, it was easy to be his true self.

Meeting Lacy unlocked something in Paul. He explained that even when it came to love songs before he met Lacy, "I would hear these things and be like, that sounds crazy. Like, that's not the way human beings feel about each other... And I had had previous girlfriends and people I cared about and when we broke up I was just like: okay. You know, I was never really distraught about that." Meanwhile, he misses Lacy pretty much every moment they aren't together. This is new. This is love. He tells her all the time that she changed his life.

It's hard not to long for a version of this story where Paul simply asked for a divorce before moving forward with Lacy. If he hadn't had such a "stick it out" mindset, the fallout wouldn't have been so messy and painful. His daughter wouldn't feel so conflicted toward him. His son wouldn't have had to stay in an Airbnb to avoid meeting Lacy when he came to visit. But Paul's people-pleasing personality mixed with his dubious conception of marriage led to a perfect storm. Before he left he would think things like, "Am I going to end up hating my kids because I'm sticking [it out] for my kids? Am I going to end up hating my wife, who I don't hate right now?" Luckily, it never got to that point because he met a woman at a coffee shop and her mom ended his marriage for him. Something he might not have had the strength to do on his own.

Paul had spent the majority of his life focusing on sustaining a certain image. Now that that image has been blown to smithereens, he can focus on something else: his own happiness. It's a route he hopes his own kids don't take as long to figure out. When he thinks about what he wants his children to believe about marriage, he shared, "Love is a very real thing. And until you experience that, you might not believe it... I would feel terrible for them if they didn't ever get to experience what it's like to really be in love with someone." Even if they have to get divorced first to find it.

I've often wondered if our high divorce rates signal something essential about marriage. Is it too lofty of a goal? Is the reality of being married not actually sustainable for most people? But as I've dived into the research and seen the divorce rate go down over time, I think the biggest contributor to these worrisome statistics is not something inherent about human nature. Instead, it's more likely the expectation that everyone needs to get married, they need to be married a certain way, and they need to do it by a certain time.

This thought process led older generations to pair up with people more out of necessity than compatibility, which later led to unhappy marriages or divorce. Good marriages grow from a desire to build something together, to share your life and heart with one another, and to earnestly practice the commitment that comes from love— even with all the sacrifices and hardship that come with it. Good marriages don't grow from societal pressure to follow a certain path. I don't think being married to the same person forever is too lofty of a goal—if things go according to plan and that's what you want for your life. But that simply isn't the case for everyone, which is why

I believe the best way to improve divorce rates is to stop forcing people to get married and to stop societally favoring married couples over everyone else. Marriage works best when it is a continuous choice—not a necessity.

Nicole seemed to agree with my line of thinking and shared, "I don't think that marriage is for everyone. I think that most people are going to try it because that's what they think they're supposed to do." But trying out a lifetime commitment because you think you *should* isn't a great way to live your life. Nicole believes marriage is only the right decision "for people who are willing to do what it takes to make it work for the benefit of having a lifetime partner." For some, the benefit of that lifestyle isn't worth the cost. For others, it's a no-brainer. And for the rest of us who aren't so sure, the legal system (mostly) lets us try it out to see how it fits.

Reconceptualizing how we think about divorce won't prevent people from having their hearts broken or their bank accounts drained. It won't allow anyone to bypass their grief or jump ahead in their healing. But I do think changing the way we talk about divorce might lead to fewer people being stuck in unhappy marriages. And the fewer unhappy married people we know, the better association we'll have with the entire institution. I no longer think the opposite of a good marriage is divorce. I think the real opposite of a good marriage is a bad one. And we don't have to stay in those anymore.

As we wrap this thing up, here are some final questions to explore:

QUESTIONS TO ASK YOURSELF:

- What has my environment taught me to believe about divorce? Do I still agree?
- What are my deal-breakers in a marriage? What lines cannot be crossed?
- Do I believe there is still value in marriages that ultimately end in divorce? Why or why not?

QUESTIONS TO ASK YOUR PARTNER:

- Do you have a "stick it out" mindset when it comes to marriage? If so, what's your reasoning?
- Are there any preventive measures we want to put in place now to avoid divorce?
- Do you think it is possible for two people to get divorced and still respect and care for each other? Why or why not?

We're officially at the end. All we have to do now is tie up some loose ends and briefly research the divorce laws of wherever we live. (Never hurts to be prepared!)

CONCLUSION:
I VOW (TO DO MY BEST)

Something I've thought a lot about while writing this book is the concept of commitment and how much we value people who stick to their word. Our society is based on the understanding that if I promise you this action or item or emotion, you can trust that I will deliver it. Without that trust, basic interactions like handing your waiter your credit card or dropping your child off at school begin to break down. What really separates modern marriage from other long-term, cohabitating partnerships is that extra layer of public commitment. Even if you don't have a big wedding full of rituals and religion, you still have to say vows and sign a legal contract to become spouses. With that comes an implicit understanding that when two people get married they are *committing* to a lifetime together. So if they don't make it all the way, are they somehow reneging on their word? That very thing that we all care about so much?

Maybe. Or maybe we are focusing on the wrong thing. Maybe it makes more sense to publicly and privately commit to a certain *type* of marriage instead of marriage itself. Because if we are all committing to the mere institution, then we're shit out of luck when things get bad or people change. But if we are committing to a specific type of marriage, then suddenly there's far more freedom in how we can proceed. We are no longer expected to stay if the dynamics suddenly (or slowly) don't live up to our agreement. If I vowed to commit to a marriage filled with mutual respect, romantic love and lots of laughter, and I am now in a marriage where there is no respect, love or laughter, then what I am walking away from is something I never committed to in the first place. (I love a loophole!)

But getting to a place where you fully accept this type of thinking is difficult. As much as I wanted to completely deconstruct modern marriage down to its bare necessities, it's impossible to ignore the rich—and problematic—history of marriage. There is so much tied up in what it means on cultural, social, economic, and religious levels that unless you emerged from the woods to walk down the aisle, you're probably living with a fair amount of marriage bias. And that bias can lead us to believe that we have to fit ourselves into a preordained social arrangement in order to be "properly" married. But as we've seen throughout this book, no two marriages are exactly the same. There are open marriages. There are monogamous marriages. There are dual income marriages and single income marriages. There are sexually passionate marriages and marriages where sex isn't a priority. There are interfaith marriages and marriages based on a shared religious belief. There are… Never mind. I think you get it at this point.

For an anxious mind, it might be distressing to learn that we can create our own rules when it comes to marriage rather than follow a step-by-step guide. But I think the true value of modern marriage is getting to build your own definition of what it actually means to be married. We are no longer beholden to the same gender roles or financial limitations of marriages of yore (or the 1960s). In Western society at least, marriage has shifted from a requirement to a choice. And not just the choice of whether to get married, but the choice of what kind of marriage to build together.

So that is what I urge you to do. Sit down with your partner and create your own meaning for this huge commitment. Explicitly define the terms and expectations of your marriage. And then allow space for those to grow and change. When things inevitably get tricky, return to the toolbox this book and your own life experience has given you. Breathe and repeat. Doing all of this won't protect you from ever getting divorced, but it will set you up to give marriage your best shot. And as our various experts have suggested, that's really all we can fairly ask of each other.

Preparing for my marriage to John was interesting to say the least. As time went by and the hurt of my broken engagement started to fade, I found myself slipping back into old habits. Sure, marriage is hard, but *my* marriage will last forever! The lack of fear I felt as I prepared for my wedding day scared me. Was I being delusional? I just spent nearly two years learning all the ways marriage can go wrong or harm your life. I spoke to people who were *certain* they would never get divorced only to find themselves single again. Yet, here I was, once again convinced that mine will be different.

But I've come to see that, at least for me, having faith in my marriage is what allows me to fully sink into it. While others might find comfort in knowing there is a way out, my comfort comes from knowing neither one of us can simply walk away. Marriage might be just a piece of paper for certain people or a total sham to others. And they would be right because marriage is very much what we make it. But, for me, it is my greatest accomplishment.

I have wanted to be married my entire life and now I am. The fact that I delivered on that promise, despite all the bullshit and horror I had to go through to get here, is proof that I care about myself. I knew what I wanted, and I went for it. Risks and all. I wondered if after the big day the magic would burst, and everything would feel the same. But it doesn't. In addition to all the fun parts like getting to say "my husband" and endlessly looking at the gold band on John's finger, our relationship feels different. We are more embedded. We have achieved a new level of connection and interdependence that feels, perhaps counterintuitively, exciting in its stability. He is my family now and that was really what I wanted this whole time. To have someone I could depend on in the same way I've only ever depended on my parents and sister.

Getting married didn't solve all my problems, though.

I still have a complicated relationship with sex and I still endlessly worry about money. I am scared to have children and I don't even know if I will biologically be able to. My contamination OCD continues to dictate my behavior far more than I would like. And I still hate most vegetables despite being a vegetarian. But all we can do is try to construct the life we want for ourselves, piece by piece. Getting married is the right foundation for the type of life that I personally want to build.

What I don't know is if it will be the right foundation forever. That is perhaps my biggest takeaway from this entire investigation. I no longer judge marriage on its longevity. I judge it by the role it fills in your life. Right now, it fills a big one for me. I just can't assume it will always feel that way. There might come a day where being married is no longer additive but draining. We might reach a point of no return—even if that is impossible to imagine in the glow of being newlyweds. And if that happens, we might have to let each other go.

But that ending wouldn't erase what we have today. It wouldn't mean none of this was worth it. I will never regret marrying John because I can't possibly regret how safe and loved I feel right now. I might regret certain decisions we make down the line or things I should never have said or didn't say. But how can I regret allowing myself to experience the very thing that I have been most curious about my entire life? I simply can't. And that, is a big relief.

RESOURCES

AFFORDABLE RESOURCES

Websites:

www.ourrelationship.com
A lower cost, self-driven online program that helps couples through an IBCT lens.

www.centerformodernrelationships.com/media
Get a free download of the Sexual Communication Handbook with over 200 questions for you and your partner along with other resources.

www.gottman.com
The Gottman Institute includes a variety of resources including webinars and the Gottman Relationship Adviser, which is a self-paced tool for couples to use together.

Books:

I Want This to Work: An Inclusive Guide to Navigating the Most Difficult Relationship Issues We Face in the Modern Age by Elizabeth Earnshaw. Earnshaw, LMFT, CGT.

Come as You Are: The Surprising New Science that Will Transform Your Sex Life by Emily Nagoski, PhD.

Podcast:

Where Should We Begin? with Esther Perel
Celebrated psychotherapist Esther Perel lets listeners inside her couples therapy sessions in this groundbreaking podcast, available wherever you listen.

RESOURCES FOR ABUSIVE RELATIONSHIPS

The National Domestic Violence Hotline
1-800-799-7233 (SAFE)
www.ndvh.org

RAINN (Rape, Abuse & Incest National Network)
rainn.org
The largest anti-sexual violence organization in the U.S.

Domestic Violence Resource Network
https://www.acf.hhs.gov/ofvps/fv-centers
Visit this site for more local and community-based resources.

REFERENCES

INTRODUCTION

"I Do Not: Gen Z, Millennials Shifting Expectations about Marriage in 2023." Thriving Center of Psychology, June 23, 2023. thrivingcenterofpsych.com/blog/millennials-gen-z-marriage-expectations-statistics.

CHAPTER 1

Wang, Wendy. "The U.S. Marriage Rate Rebounds to Its Pre-Pandemic Level." Institute for Family Studies. September 15, 2023. ifstudies.org/blog/the-us-marriage-rate-rebounds-to-its-pre-pandemic-level.

Blaff, Ari. "U.S. Marriage Rate Has Declined 60 Percent Since 1970, Study Shows." *National Review*. February 25, 2023. www.nationalreview.com/news/u-s-marriage-rate-has-declined-60-percent-since-1970-study-shows.

McCain, Abby. "20+ Trending U.S. Wedding Industry Statistics [2023]: How Big is The Wedding Industry." Zippia.com. March 14, 2023. www.zippia.com/advice/wedding-industrystatistics.

Manning, Kathleen. "What is the History of Marriage?" *U.S. Catholic.* October 9, 2012. uscatholic.org/articles/201210/what-is-the-history-of-marriage.

Forrest, Kim. "The (Surprising!) History of the White Wedding Dress." WeddingWire. March 12, 2019. www.weddingwire.com/wedding-ideas/white-wedding-dress-history.

Finkel, Eli J. "The All-or-Nothing Marriage." *New York Times.* February 14, 2014. www.nytimes.com/2014/02/15/opinion/sunday/the-all-or-nothing-marriage.html.

O'Connell-Domenech, Alejandra. "Why Most Women Still Take Their Husband's Last Name." *The Hill.* October 13, 2023. thehill.com/changing-america/respect/equality/4249567-women-change-names-marriage.

Tracey, Janey. "7 Feminist Alternatives to Patriarchal Wedding Traditions." Brides.com. February 26, 2021. www.brides.com/story/feminist-alternatives-wedding-traditions.

Carmichael, Sarah Green. "Women Shouldn't Do Any More Housework This Year." *Bloomberg.* August 24, 2022. www.bloomberg.com/opinion/articles/2022-08-24/women-shouldn-t-do-any-more-housework-this-year.

Gattuso, Reina. "Why LGBTQ Couples Split Household Tasks More Equally." *BBC.* March 10, 2021. www.bbc.com/worklife/article/20210309-why-lgbtq-couples-split-household-tasks-more-equally.

Khazan, Olga. "Take a Wife... Please!" *The Atlantic.* August 31, 2023. www.theatlantic.com/ideas/archive/2023/08/does-marriage-make-you-happier/675145.

Picchi, Aimee. "Even 'Breadwinner' Wives Do More Housework Than Husbands." *CBS News.* April 13, 2023. www.cbsnews.com/news/women-breadwinners-tripled-since-1970s-still-doing-more-unpaid-work.

Wilcox, W. Bradford. "Two Is Wealthier Than One: Marital Status and Wealth Outcomes Among Preretirement Adults." Institute for Family Studies. December 1, 2021. ifstudies.org/blog/two-is-wealthier-than-one-marital-status-and-wealth-outcomes-among-preretirement-adults-.

"The Knot 2023 Real Wedding Study." *The Knot.* February 14, 2024. www.theknot.com/content/wedding-data-insights/real-weddings-study.

"The Scope of the Problem: Intimate Partner Homicide Statistics." VAWnet.org. vawnet.org/sc/scope-problem-intimate-partner-homicide-statistics.

Wildsmith, Elizabeth, Jennifer Manlove and Elizabeth Cook. "Dramatic increase in the proportion of births outside of marriage in the United States from 1990 to 2016." Child Trends. August 8, 2018. childtrends.org/publications/dramatic-increase-in-percentage-of-births-outside-marriage-among-whites-hispanics-and-women-with-higher-education-levels.

CHAPTER 2

Geiger, A.W. "Sharing Chores a Key to Good Marriage Says Majority of Married Adults." Pew Research Center. November 30, 2016. www.pewresearch.org/short-reads/2016/11/30/sharing-chores-a-key-to-good-marriage-say-majority-of-married-adults.

CHAPTER 3

Kennedy, Sheela and Catherine A. Fitch. "Measuring Cohabitation and Family Structure in the United States: Assessing the Impact of New Data from the Current Population Survey." *Demography,* *49*(4), 1479–1498. read.dukeupress.edu/demography/article-abstract/49/4/1479/169758/Measuring-Cohabitation-and-Family-Structure-in-the.

Saraiva, Augusta and Paulina Cachero. "Gen Z Couples Are Shacking Up at Record Rates." *Bloomberg.* March 15, 2023. www.bloomberg.com/news/articles/2023-03-15/inflation-pushes-gen-z-couples-to-move-in-together-at-record-rates.

Ingraham, Christopher. "Married People Have Happier, Healthier Relationships Than Unmarried Couples Who Live Together, Data

Show." *Washington Post*. November 20, 2019. www.washingtonpost.com/business/2019/11/20/married-people-have-happier-healthier-relationships-than-unmarried-couples-who-live-together-data-show/.

Luscombe, Belinda. "More People Think It's Fine for Unwed Couples to Live Together. Here's Why Many Still Think Marriage Is Better." *Time*. November 6, 2019. time.com/5718695/marriage-living-together-pew-research.

CHAPTER 4

"Millennials in Adulthood." Pew Research Center. March 7, 2014. www.pewresearch.org/social-trends/2014/03/07/millennials-in-adulthood.

Barroso, Amanda, Kim Parker and Jesse Bennett. "As Millennials Near 40, They're Approaching Family Life Differently Than Previous Generations." Pew Research Center. May 27, 2020. www.pewresearch.org/social-trends/2020/05/27/as-millennials-near-40-theyre-approaching-family-life-differently-than-previous-generations.

Tuovila, Alicia. "Happily Married? You May Still Want to File Taxes Separately." Investopedia. February 28, 2024. www.investopedia.com/articles/tax/08/file-seperately.asp#:~:text=Though%20most%20married%20couples%20file,eligible%20for%20substantial%20itemizable%20deductions.

CHAPTER 5

Lepore, Meredith. "This Is the Average Length of a Relationship Before Marriage." *Brides*. October 19, 2023. www.brides.com/story/this-is-how-long-most-couples-date-before-getting-married.

CHAPTER 6

De Vise, Daniel. "Americans Are Waiting Longer and Longer to Get Married." *The Hill*. June, 5, 2023. thehill.com/homenews/statewatch/4032467-americans-are-waiting-longer-and-longer-to-get-married.

Stanford, Eleanor. "13 Questions to Ask Before Getting Married." *New York Times*. March 24, 2016. www.nytimes.com/interactive/2016/03/23/fashion/weddings/marriage-questions.html.

"The Link Between Money and Mental Health." Mind.org. 2022. www.mind.org.uk/information-support/tips-for-everyday-living/money-and-mental-health/the-link-between-money-and-mental-health.

CHAPTER 7

Gaspard, Terry. "Timing Is Everything When It Comes to Marriage Counseling." *Huffington Post*. July 14, 2016. www.huffpost.com/entry/timing-is-everything-when_b_7798314.

"Strong Relationships, Strong Health." *Better Health Channel*. www.betterhealth.vic.gov.au/health/healthyliving/Strong-relationships-strong-health.

"Bad Marriage, Broken Heart?" MSUToday. November 19, 2014. msutoday.msu.edu/news/2014/bad-marriage-broken-heart.

"Does Insurance Cover Couples Therapy?" The Couples Center. October 28, 2022. www.thecouplescenter.org/does-insurance-cover-couples-therapy.

CHAPTER 8

Fletcher, Jenna. "How Often Should Couples Have Sex?" *Medical News Today*. May 25, 2022. www.medicalnewstoday.com/articles/how-often-do-couples-have-sex#affecting-factors.

Emery, Gene. "Seniors Want Sex—And They Get It, Study Finds." *Reuters*. August 22, 2007. www.reuters.com/article/health-aging-sex-dc-idUKN2243586120070822.

CHAPTER 10

Luscombe, Belinda. "The Divorce Rate Is Dropping. That May Not Actually Be Good News." *Time*. November 26, 2018. time.com/5434949/divorce-rate-children-marriage-benefits.

Bieber, Christy. "Revealing Divorce Statistics in 2024." *Forbes*. January 8, 2024. www.forbes.com/advisor/legal/divorce/divorce-statistics.

Richards, Libby, Melissa Franks and Rosie Shrout. "Married Men Are Healthier Than Everyone Else. Here's Why They Get the Best End of the Deal." *Fortune*. January 13, 2023. fortune.com/2023/01/13/why-are-married-men-healthier-on-average-women-gender-research.

Buscho, Ann Gold. "The Real Long-Term Physical and Mental Health Effects of Divorce." *Psychology Today*. August 16, 2022. www.psychologytoday.com/us/blog/better-divorce/202208/the-real-long-term-physical-and-mental-health-effects-divorce.

Reynolds, Leslie. "Remarriage Rate in the U.S.: Geographic Variation, 2019." The National Center for Family & Marriage Research at Bowling Green State University. bgsu.edu/ncfmr/resources/data/family-profiles/reynolds-remarriaage-US-geographic-variation-2019-fp-21-18.html.

ACKNOWLEDGMENTS

There are so many people to thank when it comes to this book, but I have to start with my Writers House agent, Stacy Testa. You have helped shepherd this thing since our very first phone call about it and never gave up—despite some sizable road bumps along the way. I can say quite confidently that this book wouldn't exist without your support and tenacity.

I also owe a huge thank-you to my editor, Grace Towery, and my whole team at Hanover Square Press. Grace, you saw the bones of what I had and turned it into something much, much better. I'm so lucky to have had your input, insight and reality TV suggestions.

Another thank-you to my manager, Matt Sadeghian. If there is one constant throughout my career, it has been you. Thank you for always encouraging me to follow what I find interesting.

To all the experts who gave me their time and knowledge: this book would be nothing without you. Or, at least, nothing of value. Thank you so much to Arielle Kuperberg, Jennifer Randles, Christopher Riano, Jessica Baum, Dr. Shelly Collins, Elizabeth Earnshaw, Sara Vicendese, Stacy Francis, Kathleen Burns Kingsbury, Dominique Broadway, Marguerita Cheng, Simone Humphrey, Signe Simon, Kathleen Eldridge, Dr. Nikki Coleman, Dr. Catalina Lawsin, Michelle Herzog, Melissa Moya, Esther Boykin, Renee Bauer, Nicole Sodoma and Sandy K. Roxas. Your insights have changed my life and I know they will change many more.

I am also eternally grateful to all the people who let me into their lives and marriages. While your true identities will remain a mystery to the readers, I will never forget who you are and what you told me. Even if some of our Zoom connections were a bit shaky.

Let me also say thank you to Emily Parsons who helped me not only transcribe dozens of interviews but shared her valuable opinion in terms of what information to focus on.

And finally, to my family. Mom and Dad, you really set the bar high when it comes to this whole marriage thing. Thank you for providing such a great example while also letting me navigate my own path. (And pushing me along during the times I wanted to give up.)

Last but not least, I guess I should probably thank my husband, John Blakeslee, for making my dream of being married come true and for proving me right: being married to you is awesome.